I0462233

Influencing Environments and Outcomes

The Secrets To Releasing The Power Within You.

Brighton Ngarava

ISBN-13:978-1540457059
ISBN-10:1540457052

First Edition: November 2016

* * *

I would like to give special thanks and praise to The One and only
Yhvah and all the people who have mentored and supported me on
this journey. I owe all my past, current and future successes to the
knowledge you willingly passed down to me. You were all glad to
freely teach me and I gladly share with the rest of the world the
wonderful truths I now know. No storm can wash away, no sea can
drown what your time, minds and lives have passed down to me.
Thank you.

* * *

Brighton Ngarava

C O N T E N T S

Brighton Ngarava

FOREWORD

* * *

Brighton Ngarava

Influencing Environments and Outcomes
'The Secret to Releasing The Power Within'

* * *

If you can increase your influence you can increase your
networth. The purpose of this book is to show you the power
within you and how to unleash that power and potential. The
purpose of this book is to release your ability to influence
environments and outcomes. You cannot have a certain level of
success or influence without an apprehension of that success and
influence first. You attain it first by your thinking and
afterwards it follows that those things become visible, tangible
and experiential. By reading and applying this book it is my
hope that you develop a strong, functional wealthy and
abundant mindset, millionaire character, vocabulary and

attitude. If one's definition of wealth is to be limited to numbers and monetary values that one accumulates through his labors and efforts it must be clearly noted that one who uses such standards of measurement is truly and in almost every sense of the word itself bankrupt. However it must be noted that everyone who is successful is so as a result of their ability to use the influence they have to their advantage. The most priceless form of wealth lies in one's ability to control environments and outcomes.If you can 'impregnate' any atmosphere with a certain seed that atmosphere will produce after the seed that you planted, so this means that if you can put certain thoughts and ideas into an atmosphere then that atmosphere will produce after the kind and type of thought seed planted in it. If you can master this principle it means you can have anything you want in this world. You can design the kind of relationships, the kind of marriage, the kind of job and the kind of environments you want to live in and enjoy.

Many of the disruptions we face in and throughout life which oft frustrate and inhibit our growth are as a result of a desultory approach to the very things that will most likely form a pleasurable existence for us.

Failure to plan is imminent failure when they could naturally be more. Many people merely exist; they waste precious air by breathing it; they exist day by day in a perpetual state of unattained dreams and failure which is truly unfortunate, no human being has to endure such agonizing circumstances. You were designed and created to be a functional and successful being; this information becomes that story changer that offers you a way out of your current circumstance and paves way to desired outcomes.

Information is a way of escape; through this information you will be liberated or at least have the keys that may open the invisible prison doors that have been keeping you from becoming your true self. I wrote this book for the millions of people out there who want advance in every sense of the word in their career, relationships or grow their gifts, talents and abilities. It is for people who want to revolutionize their business culture, or simply improve their relationships. It is for everyone out there who is tired of being tired of the way things are and for anyone hungry and bold enough to make and leave a mark wherever they are.

I have been in the lowest of lows with no income; I have lived in poverty, poverty being a state of existence wherein one does not have a dream or a goal worth pursuing. I have been poor, in a state of existence without purpose until I was somewhat coerced by harsh realities to make the initial step that would ultimately lead me to the plains of freedom in every sense of the word.

Over the years I have come to understand the value and importance that the single carries in the context of the whole whether it is a single step or a single decision, a single second, minute or hour. It is the single which is the determinant of whether you live or die, thrive or wither or succeed or fail. Thus this book will show you how to take those single steps necessary to overall growth. Dream, thinking and achieving big usually requires you to take those small steps that seem insignificant to your big dreams and plans.

Any persons's power is to be measured by influence. If any leader or pioneer claims to have power he must provide proof of that power by the influence he has. Whilst others confuse noise with power I would like to submit that you should never confuse noise with power, silence for peace and position for influence. A man can be at the back of the line and yet have the most influence that the one on front, It is about knowing who you are and understanding where you are and influencing the environment to give you the kind out outcomes you want. Though it is impossible to win all the time it is however possible to win most of the times.

The second is the best measurement of time. It is the Principle of the Single which states that the construct of anything both big and small is a combination of single elements rightfully functioning together within a team context or in a relay effect to influence the outcome of the whole or the final, it is therefore single elements joined together that completes and sustains the final outcome of anything. For example a finger alone does not constitute the body of a person, it cannot be called a body; it is only part of a body. In the same way a body without that same finger is considered a body but it is an incomplete body without that same finger being a part of it. You are like the finger and the universe and world around you is the body. On your own you do not constitute the universe or the world, and the world is not complete without your contribution into it. Having this book means you possess the elements that will join together the symbolic body and finger making it complete and functional in a balanced manner. The knowledge of the Principle of the Single which constitutes the whole will permeate through all your faculties and in it you will find elements that will help you improve the execution of single tasks which you are required to do that will constitute the whole and influence the ultimate outcome. This information will show you the basic areas within a human's life that will when focused on increase productivity and propel one to greater levels of both pursuits and accomplishment

The important lessons and truths that have built me up and made me the person I am today, the experiences that have shaped me into the person willing to pursue his dreams relentlessly are all in this book. The information in this book is what I have discovered through experience and observation about how the rich, successful and powerful have become so and it also looks at what keeps them in their various states of accomplishment.

For every person concerned about building a legacy or leaving an invaluable inheritance for the coming generations; through applying what you learn from this book you will be able to take concrete steps towards doing so. When the time comes for you to be remembered you will be remembered as the one who decided that everything has to change.

How To Influence Environments and Outcomes is my conscious attempt at distributing the opportunity that my life experiences and other people's experiences offer as avenues for true inner transformation to as many people in the world as I can, and to as many people who need this information to transform them. You can change the status quo and preserve the timeless values and everything that is of importance to you if you make a decision today, if only you would be tired of the status quo and tired of breakups or breakdowns you have had to accept as a norm in your life.

Be motivated to deal with life's challenges and obstacles enough to rise out of the mud of seeming failure in which you may be stuck and sinking in. Give up on giving up; decide today to initiate the process of your own transformation and walk out of the darkness towards the light of redemption in a near distance, start taking those steps today as you read this book. No one can use your feet for you to walk out of the mess you are in, each man is to walk for himself, even if he may have a little help to walk, each man needs walk himself.

***

Unfortunately a great majority of human beings are living their lives always trying to fix something that they have or had but damaged or lost through their negligence. In most instances what you are praying for is not anything new, it is probably something you once had but lost through your negligence or complacence. Apply the universal laws and principles that will inspire your actions and result in success in each and every one of your endeavors from this moment going forward. There are different levels of ignorance; negligence and complacency is simply one of them. After reading this book you will be able to salvage what you can from the wrecks of your marriages, friendships, businesses, gifts, careers, and your finances and if nothing can be salvaged this resource offers the hope for a future in which your success is almost a guarantee. Real life teachings change real lives. After all the best of us have fallen before but success is not for quitters. Your success today rests upon your decision to rise up and try again.

***

As human beings we can admit that we all have areas that need fixing, goals that need realizing, dreams that need chasing as well as lives that deserve happiness and success. Believe it or not, you deserve happiness, joy and success; but it is up to you to believe and take a step further beyond merely believing but know with a certainty that it is all yours and you deserve all of it.

According to my study you can apply universal laws that will ensure that your success becomes consistent across all the areas of your life which will bring your life into a true balance resulting in the increase of your productivity and results. If laws with similar underlying applications are applied the results will be consistent with the formulae. The areas of your life i.e. finances, relationships, career, businesses are like different continents, there is a common principle that affects everyone and everything in these continents and that principle is gravity. So no matter where you are in the world you will be subject to the law of gravity. The same way gravity is a universal law affecting all people around the world, the principles I share with you are universal and can reach all people across all walks of life, similarly the same principles will when applied in different parts of one's life cause success in those areas.

Most principles are not affected by where they are applied. What causes a particular person to succeed in one area of their life will also cause them to succeed in another area of their life, success has underlying factors and it's those factors that you must discover to attain success as an outcome. Do not merely admire the successes of another man without making a commitment to the processes that produced those successes for that same man. What makes a man fail in one area of his life will also sneak into other areas of his life and cause failures there as well because you are the same person in different contexts applying the same principles in all areas of your life, unless if you are deliberate in you applications of various principles in particular areas of your life then will your results be varied. In general, realizing what this principle which makes you succeed or fail is will therefore cause you to rectify where you must and succeed in every other area of your life. Have you ever noticed or at least try to observe the most successful people in your life. They seem to have it all together don't they? Their lives are so organized, they know what is happening with their wealth, their health, their businesses, their children, their marriages, their careers. At least the most of them know and they are deliberate about their involvement taking nothing for granted when it comes to how their children are raised, how their businesses and households are run, how their time is spent, how they invest their money, whom they spend their time with and so on. They are so involved with every aspect of their lives which actually affects their ultimate being, whereas a less affluent person may not care or pay attention to where they go, what they eat, who they spend their time with, how and on what they may choose to spend their money on. The rich, the deliberate have realized that they can influence the outcomes of those areas if they are deliberately involved in the processes of those different areas of their lives. Do not take anything or anyone for granted, leave nothing to chance, and be deliberate every step of the way meaning you must think it out before you take a step or make a decision always having the end in mind. These same successful people have realized that the laws of success are universal no matter where they are and what they may be doing, so they apply the same principles in other areas of their lives in which they need to see specific kinds of results.

* * *

Here is a story through which I learnt something important and through which I know you will also learn from. It is about being resilient with a stern refusal to give up your dream. It has served me as inspiration in more than one way and has propelled me to pursue and fulfill my dreams and visions without seeking validation from other people or allowing them to destroy my confidence. As you go through this story remember this, if you are to dream make sure those dreams are big dreams.

The story is of a man who had invited his friend who needed to use his beautiful ranch to make a presentation to some investors. This ranch was the only place this man's friend could pitch his ideas to a group of potential investors since he only had no money except his dream.

So as the presentation was about to commence the host who was owner of the game ranch got up to introduce his friend and he did so by saying this:

"I wish to tell you why I allowed my friend to use my house. I know of a young boy with an attitude which was larger than life. This boy was the son to a part time laborer. Owing to the infrequent jobs he would get, the father to this young boy would move from one ranch to another in desperate search for jobs and these ranches would often be further apart from each other than what one would have desired. It was just the two of them struggling through the winters of life; the mother had passed away whilst giving birth to this only child, because of this they could not find a place they could settle down as a family with a home to call their own. They would move from one ranch to another ranch and from this farm to that farm doing small jobs. Life was hard but this was all meant to pass away someday the young boy would believe. This negatively affected the boys' performance in class. Due to this instability and frequent movements, poorly dressed and poorly performing in class he was easy pickings for the other seemingly better off students.

This same boy grew up into a young man and as he had always believed the winters of life they had endured had been somehow transformed through time and chance into more pleasant summers. Everything was much more stable then than the past. The fathers' movements were less frequent except if it were to service former bosses who he had through his charisma turned into old friends which he owed some favors. Thank God his father now had a stable and permanent job which he had been working in one of the local game ranches, needless to say the pay was good and the benefits were a like a ray of sunshine at the end of a winter spell. The two were much happier and always grateful to remember where they were coming from and where they were then.

Throughout all their voyages and adventures as a small boy this young man had dreams and desires that had been gradually built up within him. He just couldn't seem to forget the days or rather years of struggles he had spent on the road as a young boy with his father, those days now formed part of who he was. The past may be a part of who you are but not who you are to become, so he believed.

One day as a senior at his school he was required to write an essay assignment and make a speech presentation on what his dream was and what he wanted to become when he grew up. He was so excited because he already knew what he wanted to become. He had already seen and lived his dream as a smaller version of himself. He would occasionally dream about it with open eyes. He had breathed the airs of his dream; in fact he had once lived a small part of his dream on the road with his father as a young boy.

He quickly ran home after school with such an excitement and enthusiasm and he quickly wrote the required eight page assignment in detail and fully describing his dream and goal of one day owning a beautiful 5000-acre game ranch. His assignment was so detailed in read like a business plan. Clearly outlining where the stables would be situated, where and how the pavilion will be built, as well as the guest lounges and houses, where his residential property will be built and where the trails would be. He even drew a rough sketch of the structures and the house he would live in on the ranch; a 16

000 square feet property sitting on 5000 acres of game ranch. He had already seen where his ranch would be whilst on one of his voyages with his father and he had decided then that he wanted it and would someday have it.

Writing his paper was a delight for him, it felt like a higher calling with greater purpose exposing all the emotions he felt for his dream. It was something he enjoyed doing. He wrote with an excitement and expectancy of fulfillment a man waiting for his bride on a church isle would have. He wrote as a man sure that his dream would certainly happen and time was the only constraint to its realization.

The next day he handed his plan for the future, his assignment paper to his teacher after he had made a presentation in front of the entire class. During their next English lesson they all received their papers back and he was surprised more than he was disappointed to see a big bold F symbol on the front page of his assignment paper since judging from the applauds he had received after his presentation he felt he had done a great job; but alas, he had failed his assignment. When his .teacher handed him his paper he leaned towards him and whispered, 'see me after classes'. The young man was more than glad to oblige.

After classes he eagerly waited behind to see his English teacher with so many important questions which he intended to ask him. As he waited there he wondered if a dream could be wrong, since his grammar was never marked incorrectly in this exercise. At the sight of the teacher the young man angrily asked him why he had been awarded an F for his assignment, explaining how he had put a lot of effort into it and how had enjoyed doing it. He tried to explain that what he had written about meant more to him than just an assignment but that it was what he loved and intended to do for the rest of his life.

Then his teacher replied, "This is unrealistic for someone of your kind of background. You are in over your head here boy; to avoid lifelong disappointment aim for more realistic goals bearing in mind your family is poor. You have no money to buy this kind of estate. Do you know what it takes to run a game ranch? It's impossible for you to ever do this, but however if you would consider writing a more reachable dream for a person of your background I would consider giving you a better grade symbol". The boy went home disturbed.

After being disturbed for a long while by his teachers' comments he later that night decided to ask his father for an opinion and advice concerning the matter and all his father had to say to him was, "In this world we live in you simply need to make up your mind about what you want", he had always been a man of few words so he expected nothing more from his father; those words, "make up your mind", kept ringing in his head, then he knew then as he had always known before that he had already made up his mind a long time ago as a smaller version of himself. Long ago when they had nothing and things where a lot more difficult he had already made up his mind.

So the following day he took back his new assignment, it was the same assignment he had written before but the only difference now was that it was more elaborate than the previous one. The teacher became infuriated when he saw the young mans' assignment because the young man had refused to listen to him. Threatened by his teacher with another F symbol the young man responded with all the calm he could master, 'you can keep your F, I'm sure I'll do much better with my dream'."

After saying this the owner of the game ranch who was hosting his friend and his prospective investors turned to everyone present there and said to them all, 'I am delighted to tell you this story as you stand in my 16000 square feet mansion on my

5000 acres of game ranch. I am the young boy that decided to own this land and today I am living the dream which I was told was impossible. I made up my mind long before my English paper ever came up. I decided not to listen to my teacher because sometimes teachers have got something to learn from small boys with big dreams too'.

The lesson here is that if you decide you want to do something, reach a certain pinnacle in your career, or have decided what your business turn-over is going to be. If you have decided the house you are going to live in, the car you are going to drive, the balance your bank accounts will have or the kind of jets you will own, if you have decided what your net worth will be or how happy your family will be and how much you will enjoy your marriage. If you have decided then there is nothing that anybody can say or do about it except watch you get it because nobody was there when you made those critical decisions so nobody and nothing can stop you, though they dare try.

Don't ever let dream stealers into your life they are contagious so extinguish them. Follow your heart, pursue you convictions relentlessly, these are the only things worth pursuing. Whatever it is that you see as the attainment of success, whatever picture you have of what success is go get it, it is yours.

CHAPTER ONE
MATTER

* * *

He who desires nothing has no purpose in existence. He who desires nothing pursues nothing. By a man's pursuits you can measure and tell how much life is in him. By a man's desires you can tell what manner of man he is. When you desire something so much, you have the fuel within yourself to pursue and attain it. Desire is human fuel. When you want to succeed so much you won't give up no matter how much you fail or how impossible it might seem to be. Your life has to almost depend on it.

Many of us will reach moments in our lives that I call 'moments of seeming impossibility', when what we aspire to achieve or become may seem impossible to attain based on what you might be experiencing at a particular moment of your pursuits. Seemingly impossible because what you are experiencing may be contrary to what you had planned and hoped for. One important thing to always remember is that the bigger your goals and visions the bigger the failures, challenges and setbacks you will encounter and the bigger the breakthroughs, successes and accomplishments you may expect as an outcome. Those willing to succeed are equally willing to fail in order to learn through those failures the important lessons that will establish and maintain their coming successes. Great men do not fear challenges and failure. I have been there, many great men have been there, and if you are to be great you will find yourself there in that place called failure and discouragement. But when faced with countless impossibility they did not give up, I did not give up and you should certainly never consider ever giving up.

***

This is how you maintain whatever you gain in your life, mans' gifts alone do not constitute the entirety of his gifts. What constitutes the wholeness of mans' gift is the gift itself and also the man's ability to grow, effectively use, benefit from and maintain that gift. What constitutes a blessing is not only the blessing but the ability to maintain that blessing. Therefore you cannot say you have been blessed with anything that you cannot be able to maintain, for in the same manner you may have gained it you will eventually lose it.

History is filled with stories of men whom after obtaining success may have lost it by their failure to maintain it. Those who have been able to maintain their gifts have maintained the consistency of their successes and accomplishments as a result. Therefore the secret of maintaining your gift is this; do not rest or be content in the manifested state of success that your gift or vision has produced but master continually your abilities to manifest that gift or vision on a broader scale.

I have realized that in the processes of manifestation of anything may lay the secret to maintenance. This has caused me to be more focused on the single tasks I must perform in order for me to fully manifest my dreams and visions through the application of my gifts and abilities. I therefore practice my gifts and abilities with the intent of fully mastering them before they become manifest in the context of 'the bigger picture'. Each and every man who intends to be successful and remain successful must prepare for that success. For this reason I care not for any mans' gifts except only mine, for what is in my hand I can grow and maintain but what is in another mans' hand I cannot.

* * *

Mental preparedness is critical to any mans' failure or success. One man's disappointment is another man's appointment. One man's failure is another man's opportunity. When one man would crumble in fear another may find reason for existence. Why is this so that men with the same constitution respond completely different to one another? Thought and speech which are the measure of perception carry the secrets to man's successes and failures. The manner in which each man responds to what challenges him is an indicator of whether that same man will make it through that challenge he faces or will die right where he stands.

Let me address negative thinking. The first step to giving up is considering the idea of giving up. When you consider something it gains entrance into you, upon further consideration it then takes up root in you, and then the idea is watered until it bears fruit in its season and ceases to be mere consideration but an outcome and/or consequence. Not only actions have consequence; one's words and their thinking have far reaching impact than mere thoughtless actions.

Eliminate the consideration of negative thoughts because negative thoughts will breed negative outcomes. Through his thoughts a man is either destroyer of his own world and dreams or he is a carrier and giver of life to himself first and to those around him. Do not be a carrier of death and destroyer of your own dreams, choose to carry life and create the environment that will make your dreams a reality. It is possible for you to live a wealthy life with abundance in all areas. These privileges were never designed for a chosen few; all good and perfect things are available and attainable to everyone willing to reach out to attain them. Dreams come true. Dreams can become reality.

It is imperative to know that there are two constants in this world; there is the constant of change and the constant of opposites. We live in a world of constants, and the only constant in this world is change and the other constant is that of opposites. If something seems impossible I keep working at it and if it is something which is beyond my ability to change or influence I simply subject it to time because what I discovered about the law of constants and opposites is that the very same thing which is impossible when subject to time and the right thinking will become possible.

The universe, as a channel used by the Infinite Intelligence will through time and the law of opposites transform undesirable outcomes and circumstances into desirable ones. The Infinite Intelligence will channel success towards you and you can maintain the constant of success by maintaining a mind of success and executing the single functions that will ensure a holistic success. So what you do when you are faced with an outcome that is opposite to what you expect is become so determined to think opposite and see a completely opposite outcome to what you are faced with. This becomes the breeding ground upon and through which opportunities for an opposite outcome can be attained.

***

***Through mind, space and time, matter is created. Matter can be designed and altered into any form which the possessor desires or requires. When mind and time create something in space it becomes matter. It simply becomes an invisible form of matter in the same way that oxygen atoms are a form of matter invisible to the eye. Oxygen atoms are matter, the components that constitute oxygen atoms are matter. Atoms that make up an oxygen particle are matter. The fact that they are invisible does not render them non-existent or of insignificant value. It is amazing how so many forms, types and shapes of matter travel through this state of invisibility right in front of our eyes. Look at a radio station, words which are a form of matter travel through airwaves until they reach the hearer who can hear them by tuning into the frequency which will allow them to hear those words. Money can be wired meaning invisible values and quantities of money can travel through the air from one place to another. The internet is wireless, information travels in invisible forms and through invisible channels from one person to another. These are all forms, types and shapes of matter. You can measure the size of a file in kilobytes, megabytes, terabytes and so forth accurately determining the size and ultimately the weight of every file. This means these file sizes are a form of matter. All these devices carry information in the form of words and numbers meaning that the information being communicated either carries a certain form, shape or meaning whose value can be determined by the source and retrieved from the recipients' end.

Matter is simply something with a fixed mass and form. In the invisible realm where certain types of matter like oxygen atoms exist, the same realm where money is wired, cellphones and computers as well as radio waves travel, in this realm words are objects. In other words the words released into these realms are matter with real values and mass. Therefore the impact and outcome of any word cannot be limited. This means that when you create something through your mind it is becomes matter in a non-physical form. When you speak words with your mouth the words you speak are not invisible as you may want to believe but they are a finite form of matter, the words you speak are objects which may seem invisible to the naked eye but are as ever present and as real as everything around you. Matter has a fixed mass and form which you can describe. Words can paint a picture which means words are objects.

Some words are simply an end in themselves whilst others are a means to an end; by this I mean that the kind of words you speak result in your absolute destruction whilst other words you may speak which are positive and constructive become the avenues through which you will arrive at a desired end. Words are objects which are vital to human existence as much as air is. Words have been reduced to just a means for communication therefore man has not fully utilized the secret power of words. Words are not just for communication but for creation. Whatever you speak creates matter which is in an invisible state which is equally effective as anything in its visible state if rightfully used. Your words are matter. The weight of words can be measured by the effect they have on the recipients. If I ask you to think of a blue car, through time and mind you create a blue car. If I also ask you not to think of a blue car your mind will create a blue car. This blue car becomes matter because it is of fixed mass and form. The mass may be lighter than a tangible car but that mental image is a car created in the mind and the invisible realm, which when subjected to time and process can become visible. That blue car created in the mind is as real as any other thing you can place your hands on.

Start using your words therefore only for good, for building up yourself in confidence and courage and never to destroy yourself or others because words are life. The words you speak everyday are alive they either give life or take lives. They become an intangible form of matter which will with time exert consequences on you or the people you may have spoken those words to. Always remember that oxygen atoms may seem to be invisible but they are not invisible. Nothing on earth is invisible. You can see into the invisible if you look hard enough. If your faith is strong enough you can see into the invisible realm and carve out an outcome which may seem impossible for you to have worked out naturally. This is what some people choose to call faith. These are outcomes they created through their thinking and manifested through the consistency of their thinking.

I have heard and read so many stories of people who have survived cancer or some life threatening disease, and I have met people who have survived horrible accidents and unfortunate events in their lives. Their secret to overcoming and surviving was their faith. When faced with challenges and obstacles that seemed impossible to overcome they chose to begin thinking like victors until they believed they were victors. After thinking and believing they began to act like victors and the outcome was imminent, they would inevitably overcome their obstacles and challenges.

Using words and thinking to create matter is like writing an exam in which you know the answers to the questions. There is nothing as pleasing and satisfying as knowing the outcome of your engagements before the outcomes materialize. This is how every man is to live; with certainty of what his future holds and not contrariwise. Attainment of success is not a gamble it is a deliberate step one takes and if one is to take that step one should know the outcome beforehand.

Inventions come alive from mere ideas to designs which can be modified and created through defined processes. What would you become if you thought and spoke only good words about yourself? The possibilities are endless. Create the world you want to live in through the words you speak because your words are matter and they matter.

CHAPTER TWO
THE "I AM" PRINCIPLE

* * *

Whilst matter deals with tangible things and systems created by and through man's mind the 'I AM' principle addresses the invisible and intangible being which constitutes man.

Being vs. Matter
***

Being is superior to matter because from being matter is created. Matter cannot exist without being. Being therefore is the source of all matter, firstly invisible matter then visible matter. Being has in self an infinite supply source of matter. Being is truly invisible, all invisible forms which come from being are quantifiable or measurable but being can never be quantified or measured.

The universe was created from and by Infinite Intelligence. It is a result of thoughts and words. It is quantifiable and measurable therefore it is made out of Being and is therefore matter. The universe is such a beauty to behold, the jewel of all creation, it is infinite in nature and no man can completely search it out. If the universe being matter is seemingly infinite in nature this thus means that its' source is Infinite, Perpetual and Invisible. If the universe is matter it is created from and by a source superior to it. The universe is an end derived from a source. It is not the ultimate end but merely an inception leading towards an end. When one looks at the universe all conclusion and adoration points to its creator. It is the product of Infinite Intelligence with Infinite Intelligence as the creator and the releaser into the realm of matter. If the universe is matter and is a product of Infinite Intelligence then how big is the Infinite Being with the Infinite Intelligence which created the universe? Through this is proof of existence of a Superior Being that I call the 'I AM'.

Through this being things created by Him are fashioned with the same characteristics which are also infinite but not superior to Him as the source. Man is fashioned and designed after the nature of the Infinite Being who possesses Infinite Intelligence who is the 'I AM'. This is justified by the fact that the being in human is unquantifiable, truly invisible and infinite with the same characteristics and qualities as the Great I AM; therefore this means that being in human carries the same nature as Infinite Intelligence from which it was created, because the Infinite Being is unquantifiable and immeasurable through the evidence of the created universe, planets, galaxies and the endless beauties of earth herself. This is proof that our being is released from a Greater Being with Infinite Intelligence; with the created bearing the characteristics of the Creator.

Whatever you create you become the God of. Lack of this truth extinguishes all the prospects of growth and existence. The human spirit dies because the curator of that spirit lack the necessary knowledge and does not know the source of the human spirit therefore they will never know how to replenish the spirit within self and others. I am me, you are you, we are all in some way extensions of the Greater I AM from whom we were derived. Extensions in the sense and fact that we all bear the inner image of the Infinite Being from whom we were all designed and created.

To be fully effective, productive and thriving one must have a continuous connection, fellowship and intimacy with the source of who they are in order for them to become the best they can possible be, Awareness in the knowledge of the Great I AM will replenish the spirit of man within him rendering him better in every sense of the word than his former self. Intimate knowledge and fellowship with the Creator of the universe will cause you to shift perspectives and stop viewing situations, peoples, events and circumstances from a purely natural and coincidental level to spiritual and purposeful. From His perspective things that would have never made any sense before make greater sense. Everyone can gather strength for trying times, with an absence of fear and resilient hopefulness as you go through the challenges that you must.

A human life is like the passing wind. It is here today and gone tomorrow, no one knows where it comes from or where it is going, none can explain what it looks like, I have just explained why that is so. Comprehension of this truth forms the basis of the freedom which every human being was designed to enjoy. This truth reveals the gateway into another world. The truth and acceptance of the presence and existence of this Infinite Intelligence marks the beginning of a free life in which you can function as the Infinite Intelligence through which you were created. Acceptance of this fact gives you the opportunity and privilege to use the principles the Infinite Being uses to function and govern all creation.

Creation, nature, human design and everything else around us serves therefore as the evidence of the presence, function and everything's call to dependence on the Infinite Intelligence.

Duplication vs. Reproduction
***

Human beings are duplicates of the Infinite Intelligence and they have reproductive capacities which are abilities to reproduce both beings and things after their infinite nature. Human beings are not duplicators but reproducers. Though a child born from a human being may have similarities with and to their natural source they are completely different and unique to that source bearing the invisible qualities and characteristics of a spiritual source. Human beings only have reproductive abilities this means the product of the human being for example a child would simply bear resemblance of its physical source to a certain degree but have the capacity to be independent and become a life source through which other forms of life similar to itself can be created. This is so because of the spiritual source of that same being.

Seasons
***

When you use the 'I AM' Principle you are simply creating seasons conducive for inception, incubation and birth through manifestation of what you need that environment to create. A season is an environment conditioned to produce certain outcomes within that environment. That is why it is important to not only speak but believe what you speak; Belief is the environment through which words are incubated and birthed. Believe is the best environment through which manifestation of an idea, design or desire can take place, the initial and subsequent step to ensuring a manifestation is to take action in creating the channels for manifestation. It is more like a river; one can change the course of flow of a river by creating a channel through which the river can be diverted from its original channel into a new one. A house as well will require a solid foundation for it to be built up and firmly stand. Belief is like building the foundation upon which your successes will be built, it is also like creating a channel through which a powerful river will flow. Belief builds the foundation of great aspirations, hopes and desires. Belief and Action are powerful as separate concepts but invincible when brought together to function in relay. This is how atmospheres and seasons are conditioned and created. Create the most conducive environment for your own successes.

Whilst most people strive to be part of certain environments or communities that were created and are controlled by other people you must strive to create your own environment in which you are in control that will bring all your hopes, dreams and visions to life. Create an environment that others can join and benefit from. Stop follow others but become the leader that others can look up to and are willing to follow.

* * *

The law of 'I AM' states that you say what you want in the future in the present tense, with full belief that you have already attained and are enjoying the benefits of having it. You should always speak in the present tense then set specific goals and activities which would allow this matter in the non-physical state to be translated from the invisible realm to the physical tangible state.

So let's say you are a writer, you just started writing but your bigger goal is to become an International best seller, you haven't sold a book yet or even finished writing it. The law of 'I AM' would require you to speak in the present tense and not only say but believe what you say. In this instance you say that you are a renowned author and your books are international best sellers. You are looking and focusing beyond the process of writing the chapters and beyond the publishing deals and attaining the ultimate end you desire, which is being an international best seller. This allows you to work from the end backwards. That is why it is important before you even start anything to always have an end in mind. When you attain an end you will endure the processes that lead to that end. For example you may be broke or jobless as you read this book, or you may be unhappy at your job or in your relationship. I would like you to begin speaking using the 'I AM' Principle bearing in mind what you will be consciously seeking to achieve. Begin to say, 'I am rich', 'I am happy', 'I love my wife', and 'I have a great relationship with everybody'. Do not only say what you would like to see as a state and outcome in your life but most importantly believe it.

A poor person may have said 'I am rich' or an unhappy person may have said 'I am happy'. These conditions at this point may seem to be unreal or invisible states or conditions that cannot be enjoyed but they are as real as anything else around us. Everything becomes real when you think about it, believe it and when you speak about it, you validate the existence and authenticity of those things when you act accordingly.

Teachings from writings by writers inspired by the Great I AM state that the weak should say I am strong, the poor should say I am rich; the deaf should say I can hear and the blind say I can see. Not only should they say it but they must believe it, and only then within the confines of time is their weakness replaced by strength, their poverty replaced by riches. Only when the deaf declares with a consciousness and fullness of faith is their deafness replaced by hearing. Words and faith become the mechanism through which impossibilities become possibilities. Having faith then behaving, speaking, acting and thinking according to that faith will inevitably yield the right kind of results for you. Those results will be the outcomes that faith presented to you as a possibility. The possibilities which you chose to believe with an unwavering commitment and full certainty of the outcome.

All things have forms and masses that can be measured through some form or mechanism. This means the true value of everything does not and cannot lie in the manifestation and tangibility of those things but in their inception. The creation and genius of an idea is in the mind, the wisdom of that genius is in the manifestation of that idea. The inception is therefore more important than the manifestation. A baby is not created when it is born, a baby is created when it is conceived in the womb, Therefore all processes are of importance and it is in understanding these processes and applying oneself rightfully within the context of those processes that will ensure and guarantee the birth or shall I say the manifestation of a healthy baby. All stages and processes are important but the most important stage and phase would be the inception. The kind of seed planted in the womb will determine the kind of fruit the womb will produce. Unbelief can therefore not be turned into believe because unbelief is a system independent to a belief system and would rightfully produce negative results.

When the Great I AM instructs the weak to say I am strong, the poor to say I am rich and the blind to say I can see He is simply instructing them to uproot the system of weak thinking, poverty thinking and blindness in perception or otherwise. He is not instructing us to change weakness into strength or poverty into riches or blindness into sight. Weakness cannot be turned into strength. Poverty cannot be turned into riches and blindness cannot be turned into sight. Weakness, poverty and blindness are independent systems which started as seeds or ideas which grew and took up roots in your mind until they became self-perpetuating. These are systems feeding on the resources of your mind to perpetuate their existence and dominate your thinking, in most cases leaving you paralyzed.

In order to deal with such mental states and negative belief systems you must create an opposing system; a superior ideology which when cultivated will outgrow the existing negative and self-destructive systems at operation in you. So when the weak say I am strong, the poor say I am rich, the blind say I can see they are simply creating a system superior to the systems that have been existing and thriving in you. The reason why wrong thinking, wrong perceptions persist is because there are no superior thoughts and superior perceptions thriving in order to resist, challenge and displace the inferior norms.

Results are inferior to processes because processes create results. Take for instance anything that may be pleasurable to you; in order for you to perpetuate your pleasures you must be able to look not only at the results you enjoy but rather the processes that have created the results you enjoy. In this lay the secret to perpetuating those same results which you enjoy. This is how advertising machines, money making machines, social machines or political campaign machines are created and this is how they grow. Growth is innovation, consistency and relevance. This is how any machine meant to perpetuate growth is created.

Whatever it may be that you want to invest your time and energies in; study the processes and create structures and mechanisms that will perpetuate those productive and profitable processes and allow yourself to simply enjoy the outcomes. Occasionally visit the processes to grease the machine and modify it to ensure relevance and continuity of results.

Not everything that is invisible is infinite. Infinite is greater than invisible. Infinite is superior and master to invisible. Invisible things are created by and from the Infinite Being by Infinite Intelligence. The universe is a measure of the dimensions of Intelligence the Infinite Intelligence possesses. Invisible which is a type of matter is however superior to physical form which is also another lesser type of matter.

* * *

The 1st 'I AM' Formulae

being = non-physical matter = physical matter.

Non-physical matter is lighter in weight but superior in construct when compared to physical matter. Use this for purpose of this example; let's say non-physical matter is ten one hundred dollar paper notes. Their sum total is one thousand dollars. And physical matter is one hundred coins whose net value is fifteen dollars. Though the paper notes are fewer and lighter in weight their value is more than the coins which are heavier in weight and make more noise compare to the paper money notes. The physical weight of anything does not necessarily increase its non-physical value. Weight is not always a measure of value. What is of lighter weight in this case and in most cases is of greater value. This means your ideas are more important in their non-physical state as compared to their physical state. In the non-physical state to you change the value of anything.

The physical state can be completely destroyed but if one has the non-physical matter they can recreate that which was once in the physical state over and over again. With time the non-physical matter is modified and improved for relevant sake. This is happening around us every day. These are the same principles they use when making the cars you drive, the food you eat, the clothes you wear and everything else you use on a daily basis which makes your life better. This is how you are to make your existence a pleasant one as well.

* * *

The 2nd 'I AM' Formulae

Infinite Intelligence = being (non-physical) = nonphysical and physical matter

What a man is or can be is constituted in what is not.

* * *

Examples of specific goals that you would be using the 'I AM' Principle.

Firstly you want to sell 10million copies of your book within the first year of publishing

Secondly you want to receive a USD $10million royalty cheque,

Thirdly you want to receive recognition and awards for your efforts,

Fourthly you want to be the best paid speaker in the world et cetera.

The best way to accomplish this would be to stop speaking in the future tense, I want, I want to, I want to. Everybody wants, wants, wants or intends to, intends to, intends to. Instead of wanting and intending you can 'be' in this very moment what you have always wanted to be. You can have all you have always wanted to have and then you can work towards making all those things a manifest reality with an attitude of unwavering certainty. The future is a place that all of us are not and can never be. However the Infinite Being with Infinite Intelligence is in the future because He created the principle of time. Therefore you must pay attention to the fact that the Infinite Intelligence created the future before manifesting it and that He can control or influence events in the future to your favor which you have no knowledge or control over through the principle of time.

Speaking in the present tense i.e. 'I am happy', 'I am rich', 'I am blessed', 'I have peace', 'I am loving my life', will cause an alignment in the universe and its properties, resources and systems will coerce the negative circumstances, environments and conditions you may be presently in out of your life and weave out the opportunities which will allow you to have what you said you have and become what you have said you already are. So you speak in the now, the current, the present tense as if you have been in the future and you already know what happened in the future, because though your body may not be able to take you there, your mind and spirit can access the future you desire. When you do that through the law of 'I am' when the future arrives you step in with a mind that has already accomplished what it intended and is already reaping the benefits and rewards of accomplishment. By the time tomorrow arrives what you wanted to be is what you are and will be stepping into already. This means when things happen to and in your life you will be prepared for them. You do not want to be faced with sudden surprises. Surprises are a sign of the greatest lack of preparation. Remember it is not only poverty that can destroy; success can equally destroy the man who is not prepared for it.

Lack of preparation is therefore a kind of poverty that will rob you of enjoyment of what you will receive. You are what you said yesterday. Tomorrow you will be what you said today. Yesterday is already gone but today is an opportunity to make right tomorrow. Your future is in your words. You create what you will either enjoy or endure when tomorrow is.

Start the practice of speaking with full knowledge and understanding of the 'I AM' Principle. Speak what you believe and believe what you speak. Anyone who endeavors to do this will become both what they speak and what they believe.

In the case of the scenario depicted below the right way to speak when using the 'I AM' Principle would be;

'I am happy now that I have sold 10million copies of my book within my first year of publishing',

'Now I am happy and grateful that I have just received cheques amounting to USD$10million for my royalties',

'I am grateful now that I have received multiply awards for my book',

'I am lucky to be one of the best paid speakers in the whole world',

'Life is awesome; this is the best time to be alive'

When the future comes you are already ahead of that future simply looking back at how things played out. And when things are out of script you relax because you know the outcome already because you have seen it, known it, and you are fully aware and persuaded that the release of your word is a command to the universe to align things for your favor. First things first, you must truly believe that you are worth the future you are creating through the 'I AM' Principle. In no way should you sell yourself short of what you are truly worth. Usually you are worth more and deserve a lot more than you would normally think. The 'I AM' Principles will allow you to look at what you want to achieve in the future as one who has already achieved it.

Truth
***

This is truth; truth is not simply what we make it out to be; it is what it is therefore it needs no justification. Truth is to be discovered by those it is meant to liberate. Discovery of this truth is the beginning of freedom and life. Men are not free unless they are freed by truth. From now on speak these goals; instruct your mind to believe them as truth, be liberated by that truth, be relentless, and live as one who has attained.

There are different types of truth which yield different freedoms. This simply means that there are lesser truths which will not result in the attainment of total freedom. There are higher truths which will ensure and almost guarantee greater freedom. For example lesser truth would know and believe a statement like this, 'you are poor but you are meant to be rich'. This is a lesser truth because it does not tell me what to do to become rich; it is only serving to confirm my current state and slightly highlighting future possibilities. Whereas if I say 'you are rich', which is an example of higher truth; it serves to confirm my future state as a current state, the next question would be, 'if I am already rich, how then do I manifest my riches?' With lesser truth you seek to become, whereas with higher truth you already are and are seeking to manifest.

The power that the 'I AM' Principle has inevitably produces and will produce desired results for whoever discovers it. However its' truth has been limited by lack of discovery and has never been truly and fully utilized by the human race. This discovery of truth marks the beginning of freedom. It has the power to free the individual who has the audacity of applying it with full belief.

Belief in self is a level of freedom that is essential if you are to accomplish great feats in life. The free in thinking become great in their lifetime and beyond. This is who you are and what you are, say out loud or in your mind 'I am good, I am happy, I am peaceful, I am great'. You therefore do not wait for outcomes of physical or emotional processes to determine this state of being; you produce this state of being and existence as a conscious and deliberate decision. It is your real unseen nature seeking to manifest itself.

You cannot wait for things that happen to you to determine how you feel and behave. Happenings around you should never influence your thinking. You cannot subject yourself to that kind of a life, it is agonizing and stressful. I do not wait for things to happen in order for me to become happy or joyful. I have a source of joy within me so I create and release my joy without the influence of external events, this means that external events cannot influence my joy, my thinking or my feelings because I have taught myself never to rely on things that either happen or do not happen the way I would want them to.

My state of being is independent from the external environment and does not rely on things that may or may not happen. It is superior with a superior environment which cannot be influenced by anything. I am happy because I chose and decided to be happy. I do not wait for things which would make me happy to happen. If your state is influenced by external processes you will become a roller coaster of emotions. Whoever is influenced by external happenings is most likely emotionally unstable.

Nobody can say 'I am' for you, only you can do it for yourself, this is why it is important to influence your thinking by filling your mind by what you want to achieve and become. It serves you no positive purpose to confirm your current undesirable state by saying things like, I am broke, I do not like my job, I hate my boss, I do not love my life, why is all this misfortune happening to me or I am always so unfortunate. 'I am' is a secret weapon every person should rightfully use. Unfortunately it has been misused.

Place a mental picture of your future clearly in your mind, see it every day, believe it every day and speak it every day, 'I am successful, I am an accomplished international conference and motivational speaker', speak it, keep on speaking it, don't stop speaking it, speak, speak, speak!!! Then sooner than you could realize without almost knowing how it happened you become what you saw and what you consistently have been declaring. Only then will the opportunities to become will be available.

The ancient saying says "As a man thinks so is he". I believe speaking is a step further beyond thinking as long as it is done with full conviction, so I say, "As a man speaks so is he". You are the equivalent of what you think, believe and say about yourself, so is every man around you even the ones you admire for their success.

Imagine what you could become and what you could achieve. This is the fact of all levels and form of human existence and accomplishment; your ultimate destiny is a direct result of what you have chosen to believe, speak and act on. It is simply a by-product of what you are.

When you say 'I am' you are announcing the presence and function of Infinite Intelligence and you are subjecting all your processes to the systems which are controlled by the Infinite Intelligence. This statement then allows you to reproduce with aid of the Infinite Intelligence.

It is important to function at your full capacity and I believe with the 'I am' principle you come with a full awareness of self. Within you are solutions and ideas which are to transform countries, communities and families, the power to change the world lies dormant within you. Activating the 'I AM' Principle enables you to draw into the physical state what lies in the non-physical state of the future you seek.

 The 'I AM' Principle is therefore in you and has been residing in you through your nature and design. It is not in front of you, ahead of you as if in the future but it is certainly inside of you, it is on your lips and in your heart. It is who you are, 'I AM'.

Release what you are for those around you to benefit, for the world to benefit and for you to benefit.. As of now you know this truth so ignorance is now left in the past, use this principle to get ahead, manifest and become.

CHAPTER THREE
POWER OF WORDS

* * *

Brighton Ngarava

Words are invisible in nature which means words live, they are alive. Words have a life of their own. Words bear the characteristics of their source. Words have life spans of their own. Words they live forever, they are immortal in nature until their fulfillment.

Many people waste words. Many people have never stopped to think where words come from and where they go after being spoken. When words are spoken from their source they are targeted towards something and are expected to bring out an outcome. Words initiate processes, they sustain them and they are expected to bring outcomes or consequences. Certain words carry meaning, values; they inspire action, bring solutions, paint images as well as affect perception. Certain words also carry in them prejudice, malice, hatred, anger, lies, arrogance and every negative thing. Words carry explanations, purpose, motivation and encouragement, through words revolutions have been inspired and sustained, through words and the value those words carries countless of men have given up their lives in armed struggles.

I speak of the very nature of words. Their source is invisible and their end is invisible meaning their source is immortal and their end is also immortal however their consequences or outcomes are mostly visible, tangible and measurable. Words endure beyond the limits of time for their source is from beyond the veil of time. When words fulfill an assignment which they have been released for they go back to their source. Words are a loyal companion to their source. Words are faithful servants and loyal slaves to their source and master. Your words are your servant, after carrying out a task they return to their rightful owner.

Therefore I submit that I cannot hate my neighbor without hating myself; neither can I murder a stranger without murdering myself. The measure of my love for fellow man is a clear indicator of my love for self. Each time I use my words unjustly against another man I take away a bit of my life early into the grave. Words that have gone out to destroy others will soon come back to destroy me. Those that have gone out of me to build and encourage others will soon come back to build and encourage me. By what you say about and to others you are either shooting yourself in the foot or preparing your crown in a future glory.

***

The life giving ability in all of us as human beings gives us the ability and power to release words that have life within them, words are like babies. Babies are reproduced from human beings, they carry the same DNA as the parents, and in most cases a child resembles their parents with particular features. In the same instance the human being who is a life giving being has the ability to give life also to 'babies' that carry the same traits as the source. Your words are your babies, when spoken they will look exactly like you, the parent. That is why by words you can determine what manner of man he is.

Words are objects. If words are not merely words in the invisible realm it simply means that what is invisible is as real as what is visible because what is visible was produced from what is invisible. For example an original design pattern is invisible in nature and its blue print is designed in the mind first. Putting that same design on paper is the second step which is not as superior as the first step because in the first step the design is born from its source which is the mind and in the second step the mentally created design is manifested onto into a visible plan, the third step would be from a detailed plan to something physically tangible. This is one way of thinking. It validates the truth, 'as a man thinks so is he'.

***

The same would apply to my principle of speaking. You would need to create a mental picture of what you want, whether it is a car, a career, a house, an emotional state, or a healing whether it is inner emotional or physical healing.

Once you have a mental picture then write it down and thereafter speak it. Speak it, don't stop speaking it, keep on speaking it and as you continue speaking it opportunities to become and attain what you have been speaking will become present and available in a manner which would allow you to grab those opportunities. When I have something I want to achieve I write it down, then I present it as a request to The Great I AM. I pray to something greater than me, a divine Being able to make all my dreams a reality through my words and faith. When you speak words in an atmosphere of faith then that qualifies as prayer.

I consider a lack of knowledge as an equivalent to foolishness. Each man must search out knowledge to reduce the fool in him. Wisdom therefore knows what to do with the knowledge you have gained. Fools don't understand the right use of what they possess, so they will misuse what they have. Fools will always waste words but the wise consider them both a treasure and currency.

By the power of the word, that word is unlocked into the physical realm. When you speak a word you set a process into motion.

We all have at some point in our lives been fools. We have all acted without wit or knowledge. A wise man once said, 'You can pretend to be busy but you can't pretend to be witty', A man's wisdom can be measured in two ways which are his actions and secondly his words.

Create Do Not Destroy
***

Never use your words to destroy others. You will never go far in life if you do so. Underhanded tactics are a sign of cowardice and an indicator of lack of confidence and low self-esteem. Words are like literature they can either build or destroy a man. Words can carry knowledge and insightful wisdom just the same way books do. Every person is an open book, what do people read when they look at you? Do they get life giving words or life shortening words, life elevating words or life destroying words? Words are an invisible arson everybody carries around and able to wage war on any situation in life. Whether it be poverty or sickness the Word you speak will bring you wealth and healing. The Word is life; life is a result of the word. According to the writings inspired by the Great I AM, all creation of both visible and invisible things is as a result of the spoken word.

Never use words to destroy others because you can never succeed in destroying your neighbor without inflicting the similar fate upon yourself. I am so careful with my words, my words are my treasures, and I hardly waste them because I have understood their power. My words are my world in which I live in. I do not waste words because they are so precious. How many times have you wasted words, how many times have you consciously used words for hate speech or for destroying other people's confidence, dreams and reputation? How many times have you misused words through the act of gossip? Be a builder and never a destroyer. What you do to others will inevitably happen to you and what you do for others will be done for you. The Christian faith is founded on the belief which is a principle that everything in creation, the universe, the seas, the wild and the creatures of the wild, nature and humanity in its entirety was all created by God from the Word which God spoke. They believe we live in a word formed and created by words. I subscribe to that belief system that the creative process of anything can be accomplished faster through the application and right use of words.

In the invisible realm words create objects and opportunities. Here is a quick practical exercise. I want you to speak out loud and say the word car. Did you notice something? When you said out the word car, you created a mental picture of a car. Mentally a car was created; the creative process was not subjected to any form of pressure or deadline. I believe the words you speak casually are more effective at creating what you said faster that words spoken with a demand or deadline.

Now move to something specific like a car model that you like. Think of your favorite car, let's say for the sake of this exercise think of a Mercedes Benz model that you like. Do you see it? Of course you do. Is it hard for you to believe that what you just saw in your mind is a Mercedes Benz? Obviously not, you have seen it before so why would it be difficult for you to believe it.

Now I would like you to say 'I own that Benz, that Mercedes Benz is mine'. The actual fact is you do own it. You created it in your mind and therefore you own it. It is yours. It's your intellectual property.

Then tell yourself 'I drive this car', don't say words like 'will' many people use the word 'will' which is in the distant future. Keep saying, 'I drive this car'. I know you will seem like some crazy person especially those who know you.

Apply the same principle with everything else you want to achieve or attain. Now that you have applied this principle in creating a Mercedes Benz or whatever it was that you chose, I want you to try it with something else; in particular that you have always wanted to achieve or accomplish.

Speaking and thinking like this allows you to initiate and complete things you have always wanted to. Many start out strong but very few people finish strong if they finish at all. Send us the testimonials. Remember, 'As a man speaks so is he'.

The way an individual speaks undoubtedly has a lasting and

powerful ability to impact that same person in their motivation towards pursuits of success.

Having said this it is quite unfortunate the extent to which people are not at all intentional with their use of words and language because they do not appreciate the power of words. He who does not understand something will likely fail to adequately appreciate that thing. Changing the way you speak to yourself and others is important as far as building the life and environment conducive to manifesting peace, joy and tranquility is concerned. You cannot love your neighbor without loving yourself because your love for others is an extension of your love for yourself. By use of words one can maintain relationships and the willingness of others to hear what you have to say, as well as become selfless towards committing to your cause.

Studies on words and how they impact the mind have shown that positive words promote the brain's cognitive functions propelling the centers of motivation of the brain into action and ultimately build resilience. Negative words disrupt the function of the brain. And they shut parts of the human brain inhibiting its function.

Words have the ability and function of changing perception of self and of other people. A positive use of words results in a positive view of self; this results in a positive perception of self. If you see good in yourself you will see good in others because you can never give what you do not have. If you do not love yourself in the rightful manner, this too will be shown in your treatment of others. Being negative towards self will result in negativity, suspicion and doubt towards others. If you for example utter one negative word you create a pathway of more negative words through which a culture of negativity is built upon. Positive words do exactly the opposite. I always say. 'Good words make a better person'.

To become successful and progressive in this world it is important to become a master of communication. Unfortunately a great number of people are in the dark as far as this is concerned. You have to be able to deal with miscommunication and you can't deal with a problem you do not know exists. A large number of people are bad communicators. Most people make assumptions and pass judgments on other people. Based upon those assumptions people make misinformed decisions and hastily dissolve otherwise potentially good and fulfilling engagements. Do not believe everything you assume, admitting assumption as fact is a lack of character and is usually malicious. A man's response is an indicator whether he is an expert communicator or an expert 'miscommunicator'.

Be intentional with your words and your conversations. Be clear about what outcome you want to achieve and always assess if the outcome is worth it. If the outcome is not profitable for building your relationships and strengthening your connections then it is not worth it. Seek to create an environment that is conducive for trust and genuine connection.

Usually when people are communicating they multi-task, resulting in a disruption of communication which affects the quality of the information. Multi-tasking is a skill which is necessary and which you can develop with time. At most points when tasks are carried out there may be a requirement for multi-tasking.

Try by all means to focus yourself and energies into your conversations. Concentrate and focus, this way you will accomplish what you are supposed to faster when you do so. You need to develop methods of hearing. You have ears and you hear. I am not talking about that kind of hearing. I'm talking about hearing through the ears of reason. Think before you speak. Analyze why the person you are conversing with thinks the way they do, because words are a reflection of thinking. Develop this you will be less reactive to what people say but rather understand why they say what they say. This will allow you to make the necessary response which will foster peace that is if a response is necessary at all.

If you do this you will notice that in instances where you would have been previously angry you would understand such a person, and where you would have normally been furious you would be accommodating.

Responding to someone's words is an attempt to confront fruits. It is like demanding that a tree changes its fruit without actually changing the tree that bears that kind of fruit. You cannot demand oranges from a mango tree. He who wants mangoes must know to go to a mango tree and expect nothing from the orange tree. Mangoes are mangoes and oranges are oranges, no amount of confrontation can force them to change what they really are.

A large number of the people I have met and interacted with get very defensive very quickly, whilst others easily attack others based on assumptions. This is simply the evidence of the conditioning of words. How words and experiences have programmed one's mind and how they respond based on their perception.

If you want to be the best communicator wherever you are be as brief and as clear as you can with your words. In the multitude of words folly abides. Do not ever be the one to talk too much. Be the silent observer, this will help you understand the people who are around you. This will help you to think before you speak.

Think before you speak, never speak before you think. Studies have shown that a human mind can only absorb one to two sentences spoken within a 30second window period more effectively than five to ten minute arguments or presentations, in this lay the power of all forms of advertising. It is the billboard you see for ten seconds as you drive past or the fifteen second adverts that stays in your mind longer than other things you may have spent your entire day doing.

This is my conclusion on the power of words. Words are life and words are death. Whatever you decide to be all depends on your words you have decided upon.

CHAPTER FOUR
THE POWER OF ENERGY

* * *

Brighton Ngarava

Every life giving source releases some form of what I call energy radiation. Energy is life giving and results in the formation of different forms, shapes and sizes of matter. Everything is made out of matter and therefore is matter. Therefore before matter was it is. What you want to drive, the mansion you want to live in or the office want to occupy are made out of that same matter.

The life of matter therefore is invisible and in the same quality and form as light, wind and as words. The substance of matter is invisible, it is like faith. It is real in an unseen realm. It is important to know that their outcome can be tangible and quantifiable. The energy you carry as a human being has the ability to give birth to tangible elements in the time value spectrum; elements that you can attach monetary, physical or spiritual value to.

Flow of Energy waves
***

I believe that every person is a carrier of energy. By nature humans are life giving beings. The things around us are transmitters of that energy; these are air, water, light and wind. Because humans are life giving beings that means that human beings are life sources and constantly release energy which transmitted through radiation by electromagnetic waves. These electromagnetic waves carry the message and matter from the source and their duty is to communicate and manifest this to the rest of the universe. The greatest reproductive ability of humans lay in their ability to effectively use words. Life has been created through intentional use of words. By the same intentions death is also created because humans have the power to give live to whomever and whatever they wish as well as cause the death of the same thing by their choice and use of words.

The sun produces its life through emitting the sunlight; the light is emitted from the sun and reaches the earths' surface by radiation using electromagnetic waves. The sun is the source of life and the light is the evidence of the sun's life.

The same is with words; words come from the source and are carried from their source by electromagnetic waves to produce life shapes and forms which are the evidence of the word as the source of production. Identifying the frequencies that allow information to move as swiftly as possibly is important to catalyzing and ensuring the frequency of success.

Learning

I know as you read this book you may be wondering what radio waves and the flow of energy have to do with being successful in life. These technologies carry secrets you can learn from, adapt and use to get desired results in our day to day lives. There is always something to learn from observations.

Anybody who claims to have no teacher has never has an interest in learning. There are countless teachers through nature, architecture, art, essays, books, mistakes and failures. Anyone with a willingness to learn will learn.

Radio Waves
***

A radio is a device filled with components that were designed and made to capture radio waves. An antenna simple captures radio waves and converts them back into sounds that can be interpreted through the brain.

What I am trying to highlight beyond the actual mechanics of the radio is the fact that you can say something from one end of the speaker and what you say is received by someone else hundreds of miles away on the other side of the speaker. Meaning words are carried through invisible channels from one end which is the source and received at the opposite end by the recipient. These words travel through frequencies and they travel with the speed of light which is around 300 000 kilometers or 186 000miles per second. So words can travel at the speed of light which is why they cannot be seen. This means your words travel really fast.

Light is invisible, the sun emits light which is the source of heat. Light produces heat. You can see the source of the light and feel the effects of the light but will not be able to touch the light itself or handle it with your hands. The source is visible; it is the sun, and the effect invisible which is the heat, what the sun releases as an energy source releases light that causes the visibility of daytime and causes heat which can be harnessed and harvested. The same would apply for the words of a man. A man's word makes or breaks him; his thinking builds or destroys him. To know the tree one must focus on the fruit; for the fruit is testament to the tree. Words are trees that will eventually bear the right kinds of fruit.

The Principle of Free Formation
***

The formation of objects through words is a law which I call the law of free formation. The principle of free formation states that words are objects. It also states that those objects are created under an environment without exerting any pressure. Words are objects for example if you say or think "house" or "car" that is what will be automatically created in the invisible realm. It automatically becomes a quantity. You can describe how it looks, the feeling you have when you think or see it and even describe how it feels to be inside it. So speaking words automatically create objects in the unseen realm. These objects and states are created without the use of pressure. The creative process does not need the application of pressure nothing in this realm is ever created under pressure. The strength of ones' faith is not in the forcefulness of his belief but rather in the consistent application of action with full certainty of the outcome. This is the principle of free formation.

The Principle of Creative Formation
***

The next step would be the application of the principle of creative formation which seeks through systematic approach and strategy to manifest what has been fully created in the unseen realms through the principle of free formation. This process requires the application of pressure. Everything you see and use except nature and wildlife are all created under pressure. Think of anything you use on a daily basis for example toilet paper; its formation was subject to processes and pressure, from the trees in the woods, to the production line. There was subjection to the design process before the toilet paper was created. Potato chips are from potatoes but they are subjected to processes within factory lines in order to create an outcome decided by the design process i.e. of how they should taste.

In the same manner when you create something in your mind what you created in your mind is authentic and requires you to take certain strategic steps which will ensure that it is realized in the visible realm. Everything that we see, touch and depend on for better livelihoods was subjected to these processes.

You must realize we live in a world that responds to every word you speak as a human being. Your words travel at the speed of light in the invisible realms and they reach a stage where they come out of the invisible realm into the physical realm in order to create an outcome which hinges on the initial spoken word or action carried out.

When you speak words they just don't go away, they linger around in the atmosphere looking for an opportune time to manifest themselves in the physical realm and through real time circumstances. This is the reason why I always advise people to speak to themselves. Speak to your inner-man, the invisible part of you that makes you who you are. I know it is important to stand in front of a mirror and speak with you. Have a conversation with yourself. The inner-man in you can only be fed and nourished by words and words are the basis of the human belief systems.

Words are information, information creates perception and perception determines what you believe in and how much you believe. I look into the mirror straight in the eye; the window to all hidden truths in me. I make it real, and I tell myself the truth I want to live, I redefine what is real to me by my words. Before I go out to encourage others, before I go and be a pillar for someone else I make sure I am that for my own self and for my own good. What is the use of loving other people when you have not known how to love self, for in the same manner you would love yourself you are able to love others and no more.

For this reason I look myself in the mirror and say, 'You are happy, you are rich; you are successful', because I know that the words I speak don't really ever go away. They are right there with me, waiting to bring their consequence on me and everything around me.

This is why it is important to bridle your tongue, it is a part of your body; you are not a part of it. Therefore no one should be subject to his tongue.

CHAPTER FIVE
FAILURE AND THE FEAR OF FAILURE

* * *

Brighton Ngarava

Failure
***

I am so good at failing that is why I will be equally if not better at succeeding. I become exceptionally good at everything I put my hand to, but before I become exceptionally good I become exceptional at failing. What is the price of success easily attained? I believe whatever is not worth attaining is not worth enjoying, and may less likely endure time and her tests. Whatever you do go big or go home. An author named Goethe once said, "A clever man commits no minor blunders".

Failure is the inability to properly and effectively arrange the activities and functions that will ensure success. Whereas success is the ability to do the opposite of what failures do. We have all made mistakes, we have all failed before that is the evidence of our humanity. Only dead men are perfect in their state for they fail not yet their body fails them. Making mistakes is better than making none at all.

Many people are misguided in thinking that attaining perfection means a state of no failure. I have always said the greater focus should never be about what you go through but why you go through it, this will determine how you will go through it. Knowing the why will determine the how. You may experience failure but that is just an outcome and an outcome is not as important as the process that produced the outcome. The beauty of our existence is that we can change the processes that make us who we are.

Failures are therefore good teachers. If any man says he hath no teachers such a man is foolish beyond recourse. All man has teachers for wisdom is teacher to all. Looking back at your failures your concentration should be on the processes that produced the result.

Having an attitude to learn from your past failure is what will guarantee your inevitable success. So we all must learn from our past mistakes. A pioneer, a world changer and inventor Thomas Edison tried two thousand different materials in search of a filament for the light bulb. When none worked satisfactorily, his assistant complained, "All our work is in vain. We have learned nothing." Edison replied very confidently, "Oh, we have come a long way and we have learned a lot. We know that there are two thousand elements which we cannot use to make a good light bulb."

Your true drive to succeed is not determined by how much you are willing to fall but by how much you are willing to rise up and try again. Nobody likes to fall, I don't like it, Bill Gates doesn't like it, Donald Trump doesn't like it, Michael Jordan never liked it, but they all will tell you that it was worth the journey.

It's not the falling that matters but it's the getting up and trying again. If you give up on yourself after every failure you give up on living as a whole because in life you will fail at times and out of those failures great character is built. Your past failures teach you great wisdom. Now the next time you meet a great person full of wisdom in any field your focus therefore should no longer be about the success or wisdom they have attained but the process which produced the success and the wisdom. Try and find out how many times they failed, how many times they felt like giving up and what made them rise up and soldier on, because this is one of the ways you will acquire the wisdom of what you want to do. By our mistakes and failures we become better people. Everyone fails at one point or another. Failure is as much a part of our journey towards success as much as success is itself.

Fear of Failure
***

Fear is more deathly than death herself, the same way sin is crueler than the devil. Fear renders you inferior and undeserving of your rights to existence. Death itself is better than fear, for in death fear cannot reign. Are you amongst the walking dead who live under the bond of fear? Death becomes an improvement a sort of promotion for one in such a state, a sad state indeed. This is what every man living in fear is like. Don't be one of those people who would be enormously improved by death.

If you are afraid of something the probability of you even engaging in or pursuing that same thing is next to zero. People are usually bound by fear, the cruel invisible chains that bind so many of us. Yet many of us are fearless in doing the stupid things that threaten our lives, tarnish our integrity and shorten our existence.

The reason why most people will die uncelebrated deaths is because they never lived lives worth celebrating. This is the reason why most people will die poor and will be easily forgotten. There are three things cruel in this life yet the fourth exceeds them all, these are sickness, poverty and old age, these are nothing compared to fear.

Poverty is never about money, but it is about values. When you are poor it simply means living your life in exchange for nothing, a life without a dream worth pursuing or a life with a dream that is not pursued. The best resource that you have is your life and that is the very same proof that you are meant to achieve something great and leave a legacy for coming generations.

There is nothing as foolish as being afraid of what you don't know. There might not even be anything at all to be afraid of but no, most human beings would rather be afraid it gives them the rush. Thinking and justifying how that brilliant unique idea you have will fail because of the current market situation is so fulfilling isn't it? You will become the excuses you make and by them you will be remembered. Which means when you are gone from the place called life which you now occupy no one will remember you because there will be nothing to remember.

CHAPTER SIX
THE OVERFLOW MENTALITY

* * *

Creating an Overflow Mentality
***

The way a man thinks will regulate whether a person will react or response when confronted with issues or situations. You need to be able to create internal systems that are able to produce the kind of responses and not just reactions.

An overflow mentality is the difference between haves and have nots. The importance of creating an overflow mentality lies in a man's ability to attract thoughts, images and emotions of abundance and overflow and acting accordingly. An Overflow Mentality creates an atmosphere of overflow which creates overflow opportunities resulting in overflow.

<u>Overflow Formulae</u>

$$OM = OA = OO = OR$$

Overflow Mentality - (OM)
Overflow Atmosphere - (OA)
Overflow Opportunity - (OO)
Overflow Results -   (OR)

You are not a static monument, you are a continual, progressive and evolving movement able to create processes and derive desired results from them. If you want something identify the processes that will create it, then become controller of those processes and if you cannot control them you can influence them.

It has always been said that the sky is the limit. I decided it is not so with my life, I define why my sky is and what my limit is. The truth is the sky is not the limit. Aim for the sun and beyond it, if you fail you will fall somewhere amongst the stars. Never aim for the stars you might not even reach the sky.

Make Your Dreams Greater; the Sky Is Never the Limit
***

When you are creating an overflow mentality you must realize that your way of thinking affects your belief system and your believe system determine your results.

If you have a strong belief system you are unstoppable. Your belief system shapes your expectations. Expectations are the breeding ground for opportunities. When you have a strong overflow mentality you live in constant expectation of opportunities that will allow you to fulfill what is in your overflow belief system. Live in an incremental expectancy of good and diminishing bad.

A pregnant woman though she may not have seen her child physically carries the evidence of that child and with it an expectation to someday give birth and hold that child at a due date. Same thing happens when you carry a mentality, it shapes your belief system which is the fetus in the stomach, and you expect one day to hold that child you have been carrying as a pregnant woman would.

Creating and growing a good rich and healthy mentality means creating a platform where good things will rest. A platform for success and prosperity is the expectation for success.

When you expect something you create a platform for its manifestation. When you are expecting visitors for dinner you prepare for their arrival.

Expectation demands preparation. For example if you are faced with challenges and you say and believe a statement like, "my present suffering can never compare to my future glory", you create a platform for manifesting the overflow mentality. You can come out of your circumstantial constraints and limitations by thinking as a person without constraints and limits. This becomes a platform upon which solution will manifest.

When you are in some form of bondage do not think according to your immediate circumstance rather think freedom, for out of bondage freedom is required. When confronted with poverty think success, do not only think it, but believe it is yours, you deserve it and speak that success, in sickness speak health, in weakness speak strength.

Let the weak say I am strong, let the poor say I am rich, let the blind say I can see. Speaking is essential to manifesting the overflow mentality. It is not what you do that makes you who you are. It is who you are that you manifest in what you do.

Overflow mentality is not from the outside in but from the inside out. Whatever I am able to do or achieve is both a fruit and a result of what I already am. When you have wrong mentalities you create wrong expectations and wrong expectations give birth to disappointments and fuel negative outcomes. Wrong expectations are normally created as a result of selfish or unrealistic agendas and only result in a waste of precious time and disparaging of relationship.

Creating Opportunities for Overflow
***

Opportunities are a direct result of obstacles and challenges. If you want to be rich you must be capable of solving a problem. Problems spell opportunity for wealth.

***

Dealing with Obstacles and Challenges
***

Did you know that an eagle knows when a storm is approaching long before it breaks? The eagle will fly to some high spot and wait for the winds to come. When the storm hits, it sets its wings so that the wind will pick it up and lift it above the storm. While the storm rages below, the eagle soars above it. The eagle does not escape the storm. It simply uses the storm to lift it higher. It rises on the winds that bring the storm.

We all face storms in life, these are regular occurrences, it is a guarantee that the storms of life will come. We should all be prepared like the eagle to adapt and always know that like the eagle, we can rise above and ride the winds of the storms of life no matter what they are.

Your greatest challenges today can be just the wind you need to rise above the clouds. When you have problems and challenges you must aim higher than them, this may not be a simply task but it must be done, if you are to survive the storm. This skill is called adaptation.

Your ability to deal with obstacles, failure and challenges determines just how far you will go in life. Most people wouldn't believe that a man often lauded as the best basketball player of all time was actually cut from his high school basketball team. However, Michael Jordan never let this setbacks stop him from playing the game of basketball, at some point he stated, "I have missed more than 9,000 shots in my career. I have lost almost 300 games. On 26 occasions I have been entrusted to take the game winning shot, and I missed. I have failed over and over and over again in my life. And that is why I succeed." Embrace your failures the same way you would willingly embrace success and victory because behind your failures are great successes. The opportunity of success is presented by the presence of failure.

***

Opportunity is identifying a problem and solving it.
Opportunity is the ability to create demand and meet it.
Opportunity is being able to build a masterpiece from a pile of
rubble. Opportunity has everything to do with the way you see
the events that have happened and happen around you.
Opportunity is being able to see a beginning where others see an
end.

Everybody has been dealt a bad hand at some point in life, but
the difference between the successful and those that are not is
the ability to turn a bad hand into a good one. Everywhere we
go, in all the challenges we face there are so many opportunities
to do well as well as make a difference and succeed. Those who
have succeeded in the past have identified the opportunities that
their problems presented.

You advance in this world when you become a problem solver.
There is a problem solver in everyone, there is a barrier breaker
in every one of us and there is a solution in everyone. Many
people, even some reading this book have got ideas that can
completely change the communities in which they live in.
Someone reading this book has the idea that will change the
whole world. Go ahead and shine, this is not permission granted
because no one needs permission to shine. The permission to
shine and be great was given to each of us at birth.

It is in great problems that great solutions are born and
ultimately where greatness is birthed. All of us face problems in
varying degrees in our lives. Some of the problems affect us as
communities, families, businesses, countries et cetera but none
the less the presentation of these problems means the
opportunity for greatness. Wherever you are at in your life
choose to see your problem or challenge as an opportunity to

become a better person, a better leader, a better father, a better husband, a better friend, a better wife. This way of thinking will allow you to see opportunities in all areas of life.

This is the secret that great people have grasped. Great people are not afraid of problems, they are eagerly waiting for them because that is where their next great invention will come from, and that is where the next great idea will be birthed from.

So from this moment think as a problem solver would. Stop telling yourself lies that it can't be done, or there is nothing you could do about it. Stretch beyond the veil of the visible and reach out to your invisible resources and draw out solutions and ideas to counter and solve the problems that you may have. Every problem you are faced with is the opportunity you have been waiting for, your successes both now and in the future rest on your ability to open your eyes and mind and see from the end going back to the beginning.

Imagine a solution for a certain problem then work your way back from the solution to the creative process of the solution. I call it the solution to creation principle. If you look deep into yourself you will realize you have enough skill, you possess enough confidence and creativity and can master just about enough discipline to apprehend the opportunities in the problems you face every day. That is why I am not for the philosophy that says that one must be prepared for opportunity, the truth I have discovered is that in most cases when opportunities present themselves the problem solvers are hardly prepared for them. For example when great disasters strike, catastrophes hit a certain area or country or community there is hardly preparation to deal with them, but because of those sudden problems response units are put in place to access the actual realities on the ground and plan a response in the swiftest of manners. So the pathway to success requires one to formulate a response that would meet the problem at hand.

Governments can never solve your life's problems; your company will never be able to do that. Only you can change your current and future state, others can only assist. Solving problems is a progressive tool used to advance individuals, countries and companies making them competitive. Millions are made, if not billions in this manner.

See the opportunity in every problem you encounter than to be burdened by it. Only losers are burdened, stop being a loser, start with your thinking by changing it.

Whilst good thing may come to those who wait the best only comes to those that act. Others have accomplished before you came along so you are no exception. Great things are reserved for the hustlers; those who make a plan, those who go out there and bring the cheddar back home. These kinds of people do not wait for opportunities to come to them, they go after the opportunities, and if they cannot find opportunities they create those opportunities.

Opportunities will find you whilst you are actively working toward achieving your goals and dreams.

Never try to prove a point to anybody
***

Wrong competition is wrong motivation, it produces wrong results. It hampers the true purpose of your pursuits and reduces what you do to personal gratification when the processes and outcomes may affect something much bigger than you. Many people are depending on you to make it. You are inspiration and life for someone else.

Don't try to explain yourself to anybody, don't try to compete in an unhealthy way with anybody, and don't compare yourself with anybody. Living your life for others can be taxing.

Focus on what makes you happy no matter how silly it may seem. If the people around you do not acknowledge what you love and appreciate you for doing it then consider going with and spending more time around people that do, just make sure you are within your legal right to do so.

Through experience I have learnt that only your dreams are worth pursuing. Do not spend time with people that are without dreams. There are people around you who do not have dreams. Minimize the time spent with them. Be not the one to find these people; when these people find you walk the other direction. Do yourself a great favor; avoid them.

From now going forward take time to focus on what you love doing and take time to do them. Those are life's virtues that are worth pursuing.

Check your mental state

***

There are a few things that I have realized that when applied correctly will determine how far you will go or how far you won't go.

What you think about yourself and others

***

Don't think less of others; be able to come up to or down to

85

anyone's level of thinking and reasoning. Be adaptive. Becoming a master at this will help you attain your goals faster than someone who doesn't have this skill. I was an introvert growing up, with ideas that I often could never communicate. I was bad at making friends or just having a meaningful conversation with others. I was a bad communicator. It was my acknowledgement of this fact that prompted me to work towards developing my communication skills. Through acknowledging my weaknesses I was aided by time and determination to become what I once was not. My weakness was not a loss after all.

***

I have a funny personality, but in my earlier days of adulthood I would often wonder why it seemed to be impossible for me to relate with others. Only a handful of people really knew who I am. Knowing who you are is important, being able to communicate who you are is even more important. I am now an icebreaker, exceptional communicator and perceptive.

I now acknowledge and realize that there are other people around me who feel exactly the way I used to feel; alone, full of life yet seemingly excluded in a sea of people who seem to be forever enjoying themselves. So it is those people I now seek in any environment to give the comfort ability and ability to communicate themselves.

I have a friend whom when I first met was an introvert. In fact she was one of the quietest people I have ever met, but after meeting her a few times she became free and was not so shy to communicate around others. That is the power of self-awareness and what it can do not only for you but for others around you. If you want to get ahead in life it's important to be able to make others feel important and capable individuals in your circles, because that is the truth about everyone. Everyone is important and we all carry something unique. What makes each of us unique is what makes our contribution to humanity valid. I have something that you do not possess but require. You also possess a skill or gift that I have use for. By this principle no man is better than his fellow counterpart.

Do not be passive and nonchalant about where you go, what you see, what you say and who you associate with for these are the virtues that shape all men rendering them either valid or invalid.

CHAPTER SEVEN
WASTING TIME

* * *

Believing in your ability alone is not enough to guarantee success. Knowing your strengths is the first step towards success. Knowing what to do is the second step towards success. Doing what success requires is almost a guarantee to attaining success. Too many people know what to do but they don't do what they know they ought to do. There is no use in knowing what to do if you will not proceed to do it. For he who knows what to do and does not do it is the same as one who never knew what he should have done.

The unwillingness and inability to take the necessary steps inhibit your desired success. You must be able to trace your steps at every stage of your life and pursuits. You can't just make it big from nowhere. You can't just wake up and have made every dream you ever desired come true unless if your dream is to be rich through inheritance, but even in such an instance you would still have to wait for someone to die and that is something all of us are not in control of.

Every passion, dream and desire you have has to be worked on. Even the greatest people you admire have had to work on their dreams. The wisest of men realize there is some form of danger in allowing other people to inherit things they have not worked for. Great men acknowledge that with the processes of growth and accomplishment comes some form of maturity and sense of responsibility. Responsibility is a sense that not just everyone has it. If you want to accomplish or attain something great it would be better if you worked hard for it or applied yourself, your resources and your abilities to get it.

The practical application of anything you learn and know you should do is your best guarantee of becoming more productive. Get into that positive state of mind, don't just act without conscious deliberation but decide to act on the things that will ultimately empower you to achieve and attain a better quality of life that you deserve.

Channel your energies on things most important to you
***

If you want to succeed in life, you should not waste too much of your time and your energy on activities that do not bring any benefits. Energy is a resource that can be translated into money, promotion, property, joy, peace, and happiness if properly used. Energy can be transformed into anything or rather the very thing that you desire.

The good news is that you have and always release this energy wherever you go and whatever you do. Energy is an invisible substance that can be shaped into any shape and form of anything you desire it to become. A focus of energy has the ability to magnify and/or multiply any desired outcome. For example contractors when tasked with construction of a big project spend more time in planning and less on the implementation process. Let's say you have a project to do, just how much time will you allot to the planning function?

Athletes practice for long periods in order to qualify and compete in some final grand context at some Olympics. Students study for an entire year only to be measured through one or two three hour final test papers. It takes and requires more of your time and energy in the preparation phase of most things that in actually doing those things.

If you knew exactly what it is that is required of you then doing it would take you less time. Knowing alone would increase you capacity to do it. Not only that, your delivery will be commendable as compared to someone who may have just stumbled ill-prepared on what they were required to do. Some contractors probably spend more time on planning and less on implementation. The point I am putting across is that preparation is equally important to implementation, but usually more time and resources should be spent in the preparation process and only then can the delivery be timeous and excellent.

Plan your future in detail and get down to the business of implementing that project. The lesson is the importance of focusing your energies on particular tasks in order to yield tremendous benefits. When you can focus your energies properly you can complete your tasks and responsibilities in a shorter period than you would normally be able to.

Idlers
***

There are many ways people waste time. Time is one of the most precious resources given to man but without knowing how to use it you are as good as one who lives out of it. That's a more polite way to say without the right use of time you are as good as dead. Wrong use of time results in a state of non-existence. He who misuses time is non-existent in the frame of time they have misused.

Here are some of the ways in this age we are in that I have observed how people waste precious time. When you engage in aimless activities, when you become a busy-body you waste valuable energy which could have been channeled to something more productive and profitable to you. Manage your life as if you are managing a business. Seek profits and diminish losses. If anything is not profitable for you do not waste time on it.

Time, action, ideas; convictions, relationships, words and thoughts are life changing currencies through which you exchange values and commodities. The end value you seek whether a better salary, better business, better relationships with your boss, manager, colleagues, spouse, children, in-laws or whatever it may be is bought by the currencies of exchange that I have just mentioned.

Watching TV
***

The average human being watches more than five hours of television every day. That translates to about an average of 35 hours a week, 140 hours a month and ultimately 1680 hours a year which is equivalent to 70days (roughly 2 months and 1 week) This is time wasted because there is hardly anything tangibly life changing that you can gained through this activity if you make a direct time-resource value comparison. Wasting an average of 2 months and 1 week every year on television will mean you would waste around about 1 year 11months and 2weeks and some days after every 10 year cycle.

The Internet and Social Media Networks
***

Within a relatively short period of time the internet and social media networks have become principal tools for communication across all age. These have become important and frequently used methods of self-expression, entertainment and work. The true impact of the internet in this regard cannot be completely evaluated but use of the internet comes at a cost.

Other important areas in one's life become neglected as a result of time spent on the internet and social media. All the time spent on the internet and social networking sights have to come at the expense of something else far more important.

All that time we spend online. How much time have you wasted through these? Whatever you do without recourse is at the expense of something else more important.

Time unaccounted for is time wasted. Your ability to balance out what is important and to pursue those things in your life gives you the ability to maximize your productivity. Time is precious, make sure you do not waste it on fruitless activities like surfing the Internet without a specific reason.

The best way to account for your time is to plan your activities and measure your progress thereafter. If you engage in any activity without planning how you will execute that activity you will waste a considerable amount of time focusing on other activities which I call time steals that have nothing to do with your main objectives.

***

According to research done in twenty-four countries reports have proven that people between the ages of 18-64 use on average about 3 hours to 3.6 hours on the internet per day. This would mean that in a year an average internet and social network user spends 1314 hours on the internet and social networking sites which is roughly almost equivalent to 1 month 2 weeks and some days per year. If this is repeated over a period of 10 years one would have wasted an enormous irretrievable 1 year, 3 months and some days.

Social networkers with low household incomes spend more time on the internet compared to those with high household incomes. Studies have also shown that people with low education levels spend more time than those with higher education levels. Don't waste time to temporarily please your senses. Your senses will be pleased but your progress will be displeasing.

Pointless Social Outings
***

Your ability to manage yourself will give make you relationships better, not only that but this will also empower you to become a better person who is more effective in what they do.

Imagine a point in your life when you have so much balance in all areas of your life. With dedication and focus you can reach that place in your life. It is possible to be that person you just saw in your mind right now, 'the better version of you'. Do everything in moderation; a little here and a little there. Your social life should be like this.

Sleeping and Slouching
***

Too much sleep makes a fool. Sleep is an unproductive state and all of us slip into that state of unproductivity every day. Sleeping in order to get rest is important but sleeping because it is something you must do leads to self-destruction. You would be amazed just how much time most people waste throughout the day.

I once did a study on how much time I had wasted sleeping over a period of a year so as to determine just how much time I had wasted. I must admit I love sleep, but sleeping is not beneficial to me. Everything is permitted but not everything is beneficial for my personal enhancement.

I used to sleep the recommended 8 hours a day and many times I have overlapped the 8 hour finish line. This meant that I slept on average for 3months and 3weeks in the year I was analyzing my sleeping patterns. This means if I am 30 year old which I am turning soon and I have been sleeping consistently like this for all this time, then I have been slept for almost 10 years out of 30 years of my life.

Wasting money
***

Someone important to me once said, 'take care of the cents and the cents will take care of the dollars'. You must be able to account for everything you make only then can you be able to account for its use and whether it was spent the right way. If you cannot account for the small or little things that you have today then you will not be able to do so with greater things.

Your ability to account for where you are and what you have will grant you the ability to grow into what you aspire to be. The wealthiest people have a strong money and time account culture. Study them and see how you can best apply what has worked for them into your own life.

Knowledge without its right application is foolishness and a man who knows what to do and does not do it is equally a fool. Don't be talker, talk is cheap. Everyone can have an idea, an aspiration a dream but without execution all that is useless. Great people are great executors. Great leaders are great examples; this is how legends are made.

Leave nothing to chance because chance has nothing to offer you in exchange. You make your destiny by decision; you reach that destiny by using the resources that you have now. Those resources most critical and essential are in you. Destiny is the ability to assess where you are and to use what you have resourcefully to get to where you want.

Some believe in luck but I believe in the power of intention. Success is intentional, progress is intentional, getting that promotion is intentional, become a millionaire is intentional.

Those who have progressed in life are intentional about it. Great men are intentional. Become deliberate and intentional from today and you will reach the opportunity you seek faster than you would have thought.

Luck therefore is as chance, they give nothing back to the most of us. If I were to believe in luck my definition of luck would have to mean; one's ability to increase the probabilities of success by using the resources available to them.
Luck is therefore a state you create for self.

Luck is an environment you create for yourself where preparedness encounters opportunity. The other sense of luck that people love to apply in their world where dreams hardly come true is when one has an accidental encounter that will cause success. The odds of that happening are closer to rarity than anything else. It is like playing the lottery; you buy a ticket and hope that you got it right. The odds of you getting it right are next to none that is why you get one or two big winners in a pool of millions of poor hopefuls. I am of the opinion that many dreams are shattered by systems like lotto. If you are waiting for a win at the lottery for you to be able to realize your dream of financial freedom then you will have to wait a long time, it might even take you three lifetimes or more which may never happen. You cannot achieve your dream and goals with that kind of an approach.

Great people leave nothing to luck but everything to execution. For all the dreams you want to achieve become intentional about the doing of what will get you there. Ask yourself the questions that matter, questions like how best can I realize my dream and maintain my enthusiasm until I get it done. What do I need to do from now that will ensure that I empty my dream before it's too late? Who do I need to connect with in order for me to become what I want to and/or reach where I want to? Be deliberate, intentional. That is the secret of accomplishment. Then plan.

***

Here is a quick summary of how much time an average person who sleeps regular hours, watches television like everyone else and uses the internet and social networking sites will utilize in a ten year period.

On television it would be an estimated average of 2 years.

On Social Networking Sites and Internet it would be an estimated average of 1 year 6 months.

On recommended sleeping hours an estimated average of 3 years and 6 months including all the in-between naps.

An average of 7 out of 10 years is actually used up by these three activities alone. People have weirder and more time wasting things to do. You would be amazed and even shocked if you were to look into it. I have not even factored in that a large number of people lack the discipline to focus on their work in the work environment and they end up using company time to engage in some of these unproductive habits and cravings.. More than three quarters of precious valuable time you could use goes towards things that do not even ensure a successful future. I am not saying what I have mentioned above is not important at all but these must be done with great moderation. Always exercise control in all virtues.

To be successful you will need to optimize profitability in everything you engage in. In this instance it is imperative you revisit how you use your time, adjust and tailor your activities around achieving your dreams and goals.

Do not be a fool. Time in the hands of a fool is wasted treasure. Strive to ensure that at least a quarter of the time you use on these activities you channel towards self-development and advancement if you wish to be leading a life different from the one you are living now. This means less television, less Social Media, less Internet and most importantly less sleeping. Reduce your consumption ratios; instill some sort of discipline within your life for your own sake. Be committed to your success by making the necessary sacrifices.

Prioritizing the Important Tasks First
***

The road to success is oft a long and lonely one. Decision is a powerful thing, once you decide what you want to attain or become in life, stick to that decision, pursue it, persevere through it, and be optimistic that when you reach the other side you will still be in one piece having attained your dream.

Don't live for people or make decision with people in mind, you will be disappointed because most people are self-seeking and selfish. When it comes to your future and success if it means losing some people from your current circles for the greater cause then let it be.

Become selfish with your life
***

When it comes to achieving your dream it is important to sometimes draw away from the pack and become selfish with your life. Take time to become the best at what you do. Commit to being a leader and an authority in what you do at least what you want to accomplish. Never be average.

Write down what you expect to achieve by the end of the day, the week, the month, the year or the next five years of your life. Do not stray away from the path of your dream. Run your race, keep the focus and obtain the prize.

Do it now
***

Get a paper and write down what you want to do for the day or whatever period you have set out to achieve you goal. If you have an errand to run in town or anything you must do this week write down what you must do in order of priority.

Divide your day into tasks and give yourself deadlines. This simple task will help you to account for your day. You will become capable of accomplishing tasks you had set out to do. This is the difference between successful people and failures, between leaders and followers. You will realize once you start doing this you will be able to build your resilience and abilities to help you deliver under pressure. Only after you have accomplished what is important then turn your remaining energy to activities which are not so important like television and social media.

CHAPTER EIGHT
TIME WASTERS

* * *

Brighton Ngarava

Get rid of time wasters now
***

A man is as good as those around him. Be careful who you mingle with. There are people who are detrimental to the little progress you may have acquired. That is why it is important to keep your plans, visions and ideas a secret to as many people as you can. Even loyalty has an expiry date. So trusting in your loyalists is a weakness. Interact with positive minded people who can empower you. It is far much better to spend a day alone reflecting and contemplating than spend a precious minute of your time with a negative person.

The Law of Magnetism
***

If you spend your days with lazy people, you may notice that you also become lazy. If you spend some time with a confident person, that confidence rubs onto you. I call this the law of magnetism. It's like a yawn, a yawn is contagious. Once one person starts to yawn, sooner than later it begins to spread to others in that area and everybody begins to yawn. You can transfer bad things and good things. Always therefore find yourself around people you have something positive to gain. Spend time in the company of people you aspire to become like. Study and learn from them. Become a follower of someone else, this is not only important, it is critical. You can never be a good leader without being a good follower. Same applies if you want to be an excellence leader; you have to be a good follower today. The best follower today becomes the best leader tomorrow.

There is always an exchange of energy through association. There is a transfer of habits, abilities, behaviors and graces to mention a few. That is why it is important to spend time with people you look up to. A true friend is one you can always learn something from. Every time you interact with people a bit of them rubs onto you, the more you spend time with negative people the more negative you become. Make a decision never to waste your precious time on worthless, unprofitable engagements and people who do not add any kind of value to you.

Organization of Personal Space and Activities
***

When you live in an organized environment it helps you think as clear as you possibly can and reduces the possibilities of stress. When your environment is balanced your life also becomes balanced. When your living space is orderly and neat it allows you to think clearer, if your desk is clean, orderly and neat it allows you to process information in a similar manner.

I am of the belief that if your work space is clean it increases your productivity because think clearer and when you can thinker clearer you tend to work faster. Things become clearer and you know exactly what needs to be done. It increases your personal control because you also feel that you are in complete control of the immediate environment around you and likewise in control of what is about to happen around you. This is all the information that your brain needs to know, you are in control of your environment so you are in control of what is about to happen to you.

Your brain can not tell the difference between what is true and what is false it only processes the information given to it. Your brain doesn't know the difference so what you do when you become organized you are telling your brain that you control the environment in which you operate in. When you create an environment you control the outcomes of the same environment. If you can create and control environments you can create and influence the direction your future takes.

If you can believe without an inch and shadow of a doubt that you are in control of your future and you determine the outcome of all things concerning you, you will certainly be without any doubts have control.

You are in control of what happens around you meaning you are in control of your environment. That is one of the most powerful truths I have ever discovered. I know sometimes all of us feel at some point powerless and without control of what happens to us. That is a fact to life; you will not always be in control of what happens to you but you and everyone else are in control of how you go through your circumstances. The environment that I speak of, the environment which you are in control of is you perception and reaction to events that happen in your life.

There is nowadays a type of farming called technology farming. In this type of farming plants are grown within controlled environments which are conducive for their maximum productivity, I thought that was amazing. I then realized if people can create a particular environment to accommodate a particular seed and nurture it to maximum productivity then human beings can create environments conducive for their ideas to grow. Note importantly this practice of technology farming now varies from country to country, and region to region and is now practiced around the world.

Human beings can control environments in which plants grow and they can even determine how productive they should be. The same thing happens to your mind when you live within an organized environment, because whoever controls the environment controls the future of that environment because environments give birth to outcomes. Outcomes are futures realized. Where you are now is the outcome of an environment which was controlled by certain elements. Whether you were in control of those elements is what contributed to the outcomes. Thus the common statement, 'man is the product of his environment'.

***

To be able to reach this level of organization and to start living this way you must from now on going forward determine your goals. If this is a new exercise plan at least a day in advance, Plan your day and the specific tasks and activities you will need to carry out if you are to accomplish your goals. You can eliminate surprises from your routine and if they do pop up you have so much focus and you have a goal that you are determined to reach within a specific period, this ultimately reduces any stress that can be potentially caused by forgetting to complete some important task. If you are surprised by surprises it simply means you never had a plan, a regiment to stick by. If you have a plan and you have planned ahead of time what you will do in your day then you will see surprises exactly for what they are.

Surprises for the organized and the determined are simply distractions that need to be avoided. If you can't avoid them then push them aside, if you can't push them aside ignore them. If all this is impossible look through and choose to see past and beyond them whilst you strive to reach your goal. You do not have to subject yourself to an environment which is overwhelming.

Many people give up because they feel they are unable to salvage control from the flood waters of work demands and relationship challenges. People give up. When people don't know how to deal with issues they quit but we all know quitting doesn't really solve anything. A quitter today will probably quit tomorrow because they would not have dealt with what made them quitters before. You do not want to be watching repeat episodes of yourself failing, stressing, quitting, depressed or giving up. These are all things you can escape through effectively planning and actively participating in the transformative processes you must go through as an individual. Scientifically it has been proven that clean environments improve and boost your memory and reduce depression and negativity. You can create your own environment in which you are the alpha, instead rather than being part of one an environment where your outcome will be affected or determined by someone else.

Practice
***

A teacher can only better a teacher when they teach. A sportsman becomes excellent at his trade when he does what he must do; exercise and practice. Regular practice develops consistency, determination, focus and patience as you grow. This will build your levels of resilience and creativity within your chosen field. I remember the first time I was inspired by a poet. I had so much zeal and fire in me that I immediately began to write poetry. I would spend the next three months writing poetry for at least three to four hours a day. I committed to my personal improvement and set goals and deadlines for myself. In those three months I wrote between three to four pieces of poetry and a short story composition every day. The result was tremendous positive growth in my creative writing ability and poetic writing ability. After I had mastered that I moved on to something else. I shifted my interest to song writing which I spent time a good while developing now it is almost second nature in me.

Bottom line is I have given myself time to develop and pursue certain passions and interests in the past and you can also do the same thing and become very good at it. Practice enlarges your ability to perform whatever task you want to. This will certainly put you on the fast lane to success. You can only be as good as your practice. Not only must you want it badly, you must also practice as if all things hinge on that practice and you must belief like all things depend on it.

Books, Books, Books
***

Literature transcends time, and all the seasons of man. Literature translates time into timelessness. What could be more eternal and beautiful than books? We live and we die but books and what's in them endures forever, if not exposed to bad weather. I believe that even in heaven there are countless pieces of literature and libraries because even Infinite Intelligence is understood through interpretation of literature, oh what the hope of eternity without books is.

Any man who seeks to truly improve self and others must commit to reading with the purpose and intention of learning. Reading is pleasurable, enlightening and entertaining.

The primary use of reading is for learning. When you stop reading you stop learning and when you stop learning you stop growing. When you stop growing it means you are dead. For death is a state of the cessation of growth of anything. There is no difference between a man lying dead in a mortuary and one who is still walking, breathing and living with inability to attain some form of learning. A man who cannot learn anything from books, friends, enemies, world events or life has condemned himself to death. If experience cannot teach you anything, for what use are the both of you?

Whoever loves himself takes time to grow him. Whoever wants to die will stop growing. Everyone regardless of background gives himself a better chance at succeeding in life when he tasks himself with learning.

Guns destroy people, families and countries. Books build people, families and countries. Freedom without education is still bondage. When your mind is free through learning physical bondage can do you no harm. For a mind freed through learning is free.

From learning emanates knowledge, a comprehension of the knowledge and the subject matter brings understanding. The right use of that knowledge and understanding is wisdom.

The worst that any man can ever be is locked up in their mind, it is worse than being locked up behind bars. Nations and enduring institutions are built on a foundation of learning. Those with legacies have been remembered partly because of their respect for education and learning. The best thing you can ever do for self is to grab a book and learn something instead of sitting in front of a television all day or most of your night. The little you know is just a scratch on the surface of what truly is. Within the covers of books are heavens and their treasures, within the wall of their covers are planets undiscovered, inventions, ideas and everything else you have ever fantasied about. Read as many as you can to be able to imagine a life without limits, because beyond imagination are avenues and possibilities for fulfillment. Foolish people never pick a book, oh what wasted existence readless minds be.

Protect Your Vision
***

Be careful of dream stealers and dream killers. In the same manner others find their way into your life to build you and become a blessing to you by growing you there are those whose purpose and only business is to inhibit and constrain you and your beliefs and dreams. The quicker you identify these kinds of people in your circles the quicker you must eliminate them. Do not give the sons of the devil a chance to extinguish your dreams. Remind yourself of the inception of your dream, vision or idea. Always remind yourself that your purpose is bigger than you. The right kind of purpose seeks to reach beyond what is immediate and within reach. If your vision is not bigger than you it is not a vision but selfishness.

The man who seeks motivation from fellow man does not have a true dream; those with true dreams instead motivate men to follow their dream. Dr. Martin Luther King Junior did not need motivation to believe what he stood for but he was the motivation of what he stood for. When the masses saw him they believed not his person but rather his message. The people of his era did not follow a man with a message but they followed the message that a man carried. Decades later the man is no more but his words linger in the minds of everyman today and inspires them to further believe that there is a dream.

You and your vision are not one. Your vision should be your source of life and motivation. It should be the reason you wake up every day and get on your grind. It inspires your hustle. For these reasons and more your vision should be bigger and greater than you. You and you vision cannot be one. You vision should become your master and instructor aligning your behavior and thinking to itself. Your vision is the device through which you will gain influence. On his own a man can have no influence, except through his gifts, abilities and his vision. Therefore the net-wealth on any man is not in how he carries himself but rather it lies in the visions he carries within him. Many empty men carry themselves around as though they were worth something. They pretend through their stature until they start to speak. Only then do you discern than they have not vision in them thereby annulling their existence.

One who has not known self cannot defend self. Knowing your purpose and defining your vision helps you know yourself. This protects both you and your vision from dream killers and dream stealers. When you realize that by your vision you must value yourself you will change how you value yourself and others. Your vision is bigger than you actually think. Do not make your vision small, though you may be required to start small your vision is not small neither are you. This realization increases your self-worth and allows you to identify your true self and abilities as well as function accordingly with greater confidence.

Self-Motivation
***

When you have a dream you must be able to self-motivate. Put your heart aside and use your head. Attainment of vision is a decision one must make and stick with. Consistency requires not emotion but discipline. When a man sets out to build a house discipline is a more important resource than emotion. When running your race be focused and disciplined, you cannot afford to be emotional during the race of life. This is why people do not cry during the race, the do so after crossing the finish line and having won. So you can become emotional but only after you cross the finish line. Emotional people hardly ever accomplish anything; emotional people give up because they may not have their way and their emotions tell them to do so. Self-motivation therefore has got nothing to do with emotions but discipline.

Wisdom forever teaches her lesson. Only the willing minded continues to learn. You learn with your mind and you believe with your heart. Do not confuse what you must learn with what you must believe for the two cannot substitute each other.

Mind and Heart Motivation
***

Mind and heart are both essential to motivation. You cannot succeed with only one of them. Believe with your heart and never with your mind. Think with your mind and never with your heart. Confuse the two you may have created a recipe for disaster. You need to understand the power of the heart and the power of the mind. Understanding these two would yield amazing dividend for you. Combine heart and mind. Believe as if faith is the only way to attainment and think, act and work like your accomplishments only depend on your hard work. When these two are combined the synergy with be fruitful.

CHAPTER NINE
VALUE DIFFERENCES

* * *

Value Differences
***

People dissolve valuable partnerships, marriages, relationships because they fail to value differences.

The greatest conflicts arise from the fact that one party wants the other to see things, feel and reason the way they do. I always say nothing is impossible but this is absolutely impossible. Everybody has prior experiences and encounters that influence their decision making. Past experiences and encounters become influential in the decision making processes. That is why it is important to value differences in opinion with everybody in your life circles. Because the first step to understanding and influencing other peoples' decision making is knowing what causes and influences those people to reason and act the way they do.

There is always a better way of getting exactly or an outcome close to what you want in any situation if you are wise enough. Do not force people to see things or reason the way you do.

This will cause conflicts and tensions which may be unnecessary.

The way all of us process information varies based on how we have been somewhat subjectively exposed to information in the past. That is what I call an environment.

Environments
***

Environments are the conditions in which and through which ideas, information and belief systems are communicated to an individual or a group of people. When received it ultimately influences perception and behavior according to the conditioning of the source of that environment. Your best bet of winning a certain person or group over is to share your belief in an environment which you control. Control the environment, be the source of the environment in which the parties are comfortable enough to listen to without constraining themselves. Then you will have your way.

Value Relationships
***

Everyone was made for relationship. This means relationships are very important. Without relationship man could not grow. Through relationships and community problems are solved faster.

* * *

There are three different types of relationships in my observation that man finds himself entangled in at one point or another in life;

1. Unhealthy Relationship

These are the relationships where conflict arises from one or both party's inability to value their differences or the differences of the other party. Unhealthy relationships can have a great impact in one's life. Your ability to maintain quality relationships is the indicator of how far you will go in life. People unnecessarily hold on to relationships which are detrimental. They keep holding onto people and belief systems that are bad for them.

I have been in relationships where I have been subjected to really manipulative and controlling hypocrites. I had to grow out of those kinds of relationships and formally part ways with people I had previously thought I desperately needed to hold on to. What had become different this time around, the difference was that I had decided where I wanted to go in life and I was simply not seeing them in that future that I was pursuing. You must review the importance and roles of the people that you pay with your time and if you see any underperformers who cannot deliver as the C.E.O of your life you should fire them.

You are the C.E.O of your life, the Architect of your future. Your life is a company or a business therefore run it like one. Fire all your bad habits together with people who introduced them to you. Get rid of all the weights that pull you down and backwards. By the time you finish living your life it should be a race well run. A life where friends were both gained and lost but nonetheless a life where all your dreams were not just merely fulfilled but fully realized and thoroughly enjoyed.

Sometimes a business has to downsize to increase its profitability. Anything that proves to be just a waste of time and resources must be cut out of your life without hesitation or sympathy. Get rid of anyone who wastes your time. Get rid of them, time wasters simply pull you back from reaching your destiny, they slow you down.

Once time is wasted there is nothing you can do about it. Once you have wasted your time there is nothing you can do about it. Time wasted is waste in deed. You can concur to the painful reality that you have already wasted so much time in your life by concentrating your energies on unhealthy and unprofitable relationships. I always say, a wise man knows when to say hello and when to say goodbye.

Some reading this book are where you are in life because of holding on to dead weight companions. Dead weight is heavy weight. Every once in a while it is imperative for major corporations to have review meetings. Some have review meetings on a daily basis; other departments have them on a weekly, some monthly and some annually. The purpose of this is to assess whether the plan had been implemented and what ere the results during the interim. An assessment is carried out on how to best improve strategy in order to increase productivity in implementation of the next strategy. In the same manner things would be done in the corporate world where there is so much emphasis on accountability and consistency of results is demanded you also must have such structures in place.

Have a meeting with yourself and be real about it. Don't waste precious time on friendships and interactions for the sake of it. The quality of the company you keep is an indicator of the quality of life you are planning to live. If a man tells me where he wants to go I simply look at his friends, companions and associates. Your friends are either a part of your journey or they are not your friends at all. Don't waste time on people who are not going to be part of the greater picture of your life and success, this is why you must know when to say goodbye. Unhealthy friendships fail to acknowledge your struggles, hopes and milestones in your life.

2. Balanced Healthy Relationships

This is a mutual and beneficial to both parties. There is an acceptance and understanding that parties will differ in opinion and this should never ever be the foundation of conflict but rather the platform upon which the relationship can be and is strengthened. There is no candy coating of the wrong decisions of one party by the other party. These relationships house genuine truth and friendship. They are characterized by accountability of both parties and a mutual respect. Healthy relationships have a genuine gladness when one party advances and has more progress than the other. Balanced relationships have an absence of competition and jealousy. Within balanced relationships both parties have a mutual non spoken agreement to be selfless and serving.

3. Non-Existent Relationship

If you become a yes person in any relationship it simply means that you have become ineffective in your role and irrelevant in that relationship. If you have to be a yes person in any type of relationship you are in so that you may be able to maintain that relationship it is a clear indicator that you are in the wrong relationship or that relationship has outlived its purpose.

The Philosophy of Success
***

Why is this important to the philosophy of success? It is because healthy relationships have been proven to increase productivity within any environment in most case scenarios. If employees of a company x are united than those of company y who are always playing cat and dog with the supervisors, managers and amongst colleagues the company x becomes more profitable than company y.

If management within a certain organization do not understand the processes the rest of the team have to go through to produce a product or deliver a service the management or manager may have unrealistic expectations from the rest of the team thereby causing resentment, friction which will negatively affect the productivity of that team and company.

Friction is not only measured by confrontation but by a resistance and gradual increase in the unwillingness of the subordinate party to fulfill organizational functions, or by the superior's or managers' unrealistic demands on subordinates. If you understand that your teenage son or daughter is an individual you would stop trying to think for and regulate their behavior then your relationship would be better.

***

It not worth being right or winning an argument and after that lose valuable people and relationships. I believe relationships are so precious, they are souvenirs or gifts you received from someone so dear and important to you; the Infinite Being who is the Great I AM. If you were asked to put a price on something so special and precious to you it would be impossible. Well the same applies to relationships, they are so valuable they are priceless, it might just be the case for some of you reading this book that you have not yet discovered the treasure in your relationships because you have not acknowledged the differences the other party carries which by the way makes the relationship complete.

What is black to you may be white for someone else, it is ok. If that difference threatens the purpose of whatever union you may have then find common ground upon which the parties involved would be able to stand. Remember outcome is not as important as process but nonetheless very important and when process doesn't reach some form of compromise in this instance there would be negative outcomes, meaning the purpose of the union was denied by differences.

Always seek an outcome
***

Whatever you decide to do, wherever you decide to go, whoever you decide to interact with you must decide what you desire as an outcome.

When you talk to or decide to spend time with somebody you must be specific about the purpose of your meetings, outings and friendship and what your expected outcomes are. When I decide to interact with anybody it is either I have something valuable to learn or I have something valuable to teach.

Have goals for everything in your life even friendly engagements should be guided by goals that is the only way you can be able to measure how far you have come from where you were and how far you have to go from where you are.

Emotions
***

Some people are more emotional than others, they engage in conversations, deals, and other important things in their lives driven by emotions. This is a dangerous road to take because emotions are constantly changing and if you are to live by them you might be in for some serious trouble. Emotional people set themselves up for disappointment and failure. Do not be naïve to mistake passion for emotion. They produce the same energy able to both build and destroy. Emotional people decide today and regret tomorrow, never be like this, it may feel good in the moment but what is worth a moment to a lifetime.. Think things through before you make decisions. Remove yourself from your situation and seek to be as objective as you possibly can, then you may truly see things for what they are.

Do not entertain Gossipers and Slanderers
***

This will probably result in you having fewer friends. Most people are manipulative in nature, if they are part of a system they cannot manipulate they will most certainly find reasons to criticize. Now criticism has evolved into a profession. Before I listen to a critic I compared the critic to whom they are criticizing. I have often discovered that the motivation for these criticisms is purely jealousy. I find that most people who talk about others have a serious root of jealousy and envy in them. I hardly entertain such and if I do entertain them it is for learning through observing them. After all a fool is a great source of learning.

Great people have no time to discuss other people but focus on their vision. Little people discuss great people and try to cast them in bad light. Whilst risers rise talkers talk and haters hate.

Most of the critics around you that discourage you or show you how inadequate your dream is and how it cannot be do have no vision of their own so they make other people's business their own. Gossip reveals your inadequacies and simply mirrors the jealousy and envy you have for the person you are gossiping about. If someone is jealous about someone else because they bought a

new car or just got a promotion whatever the case may be with you or anyone else the cause of that jealousy is envy. It is simply a reflection of opposites where on one opposite there is abundance or provision and on the other side where the jealous and envious stand is lack and failure. What goes around comes around; remember that when you decide to stoop so low as to negatively talk about someone else to slander or destroy. When you slander, backbite and gossip you are simply saying you have failed to be like that person you are busy hating on.

At the end of it all human beings are more connected in more ways than you would imagine. If I destroy a human being in whichever ways I devise I am affecting the balance in the dynamics of humanity which in turn will with time destroy me. I cannot destroy my neighbor without destroying myself, when I destroy my neighbor I destroy myself. That is why it is important to live by the golden rule and in all actions we choose to remember that those who live by the sword will die by the sword. Your words and actions are swords which you choose to either give life or take life.

There is always a better and more noble way to get what you want and that lies not in destroying others but in uplifting them. I have been part of systems in numerous occasions where participants in those systems have thought that they could get promotions and favors from superiors by slandering others. Thank God I was wiser and more resilient than that. Many people fail to realize and acknowledge that there are people out there who have found and applied the formulas that cause success.

The first step in succeeding in anything you set out to do is acknowledging that there is someone out there who is better than you. Find the people who have preceded you. Your predecessors who are examples at what you want to do. Find them and acknowledge them. Acknowledgement of those better then you gives you the ability to become exactly or even more than them. You attain the graces to become and to accomplish more than your teacher. I call it the principle of impartation of grace by acknowledgement. That is why it is important to get a mentor who is an expert in your area of pursuits. Professionals, philanthropists, community leaders, politicians, sportsmen; whoever they are and whatever it is they do find those success cows and milk them like never before.

***

Think Community and Leadership
***

Everyone carries a solution for society. You are a solution carrier. Being progressive and successful would then mean being able to benefit community through your gift and abilities. Community is built when individuals use their gifts and abilities not only for their personal gain and benefit but for the benefit of others. Gift and abilities are for community first and secondarily for self. Your abilities are designed in a way which naturally benefits others. Your satisfaction should be derived from the benefit of others.

Therefore one's ability to position self to become accessible with what is beneficial to others is a form and level of leadership. People only remember leaders. History remembers leaders not followers. Leaders and inventors who were bold enough to step out and stand for what they believe in are remembered; the followers and doubters are no so remembered.

At some point in your life you will have to step out and just do what you know how to do best because someone is desperately waiting for you to use what you have for their lives to change. Someone somewhere out there is waiting on you to be your true authentic self so that their lives will be completely transformed.

Use what you have right now to get to where you need to go. Gratification, satisfaction and fulfillment are realized when your gift, ability and vision is communicated to community. Strive to use your gifts to bridge communities, if you are able to bridge communities you can build destinies. We are all community. If you have ability that no one else has use it for and in community. Your ability to do this is an indicator that your gift or ability is not limited to that community by through time will be presented before a greater and broader audience. You can start a multi-billion dollar business but in my understanding of leadership and community that great initiative is not really for your sole benefit as a founder, pioneer or inventor but for the people who will benefit from your initiatives.

***

I believe people with great success and accomplishments have a responsibility to community. Your idea therefore is not for your benefit but for someone else'. If you start a huge multi-billion dollar corporation the purpose of that business is community. The purpose of that business is in my opinion to create tens of thousands of jobs that would in turn positively affect hundreds of thousands of lives. When you change one life you change a family. Transforming a family means transforming an entire community. When you change a community you change society. When you change society you change the culture of the world.

Therefore the greater purpose of starting a business will not be to make money only but to change lives as you make that mullah. Fulfill with passion every one of you visions and in the same way fulfill the mandate of sustaining the people that ensures the fulfillment of that vision.

Visionaries should therefore create communities, businesses, companies, corporations and organizations with environments which are conducive for the raising of new leaders. You have responsibility to assist other people in your community who are less privileged than you as well as allow others to benefit from your gift and ability. The marks of true leadership are carried by a man's followers. If I would like to see what manner of man one is I do not simply inspect his product but also his followers.

The purpose of leadership is the replicate your belief and faith in others. From today start being a leader, if you expect to advance in life be a leader. Be the man and woman that someone else is willing to follow. Leadership is not a position but it is influence. The process of developing others' abilities and transferring your abilities from self to other increases your influence on those people.

Your ability to do this perpetuates your legacy as a leader. The fact that one may have a great invention or great gifting or ability is not a guarantee that that same person possesses the same level of leadership. I have seen and personally met great inventors, skilled artist and amazing people who have the capacity to become wealthy through the right use of their virtues but lack the leadership within them to make it happen.

You should always be able to rearrange self and become versatile and adaptive with your gifts and abilities because environments are constantly changing together with the requirement of those environments. Leaders grow other leaders. Your ability to adapt therefore gives way to revolutionary authorship of solutions to the same problems you may have been dealing with.

You are a revelation. Your inventions are a revelation. Your ideas are a revelation. When you are a good leader you will take time and apply strategy to clearly define your visions, ideas and gifts.

Transference of revelation
***

This is important. If anything is not clearly defined in purpose and function it will be misunderstood. And usually whatever is misunderstood by people is subjected to abuse, whether it's your gift, vision or resources. If that is not the case the very same people may attempt to manipulate it to suit their desires.

Manage your environment. Be able to create and control an environment where people in that environment do not compete for leadership position in an unhealthy relationship destroying manner. No matter how much you can talk about team work this makes no sense when structures that would strengthen and support teamwork are not in place. It makes no sense if the team players do not understand the vision of your organization.

***

To become successful and progressive it is important to understand these principles. You will not be able to make it on your own. You will need good, inspired, informed people to make it in life. It is your responsibility to find those good people and inspire as well as inform them as far as the common goal and purpose is concerned. If you place these necessary structures in place it becomes an individual's prerogative in that system to self-advance.

Normal people have desire to grow and be progressive because we are progressive by nature so you should never ignore or not take serious your personal or someone else's urge to ascend to the realms of leadership. This may differ in a case where you have identified qualities in someone within your environment that has leadership abilities that you wish to develop.

Spend time on other people; show them that you really care about advancing their lives and developing their abilities. This will separate you from the rest. This is what makes you that leader with a difference. Never promote an environment that suppresses its members from advancing and growing. If you find yourself in such an environment get out right now, you are worth more than where you you're your ability to make well thought out, independent decision is a sign of leadership. Leadership is the freedom to make decision. Wise leaders make reasoned out decisions.

There is no true growth without error. Mistakes make the best teachers. Don't beat yourself up for your mistakes, learn from them. Mistakes are not bad; they are a sign of decision making ability. I do not know anything more detrimental to a person that makes no mistakes than not making mistakes. I have realized that you cannot judge results alone even though results may be an indicator of the type of processes that created the results.

People who believe in a world where err exists not are preliterate. Focusing on results does not change results. Judge rather a man's action. For if you can intercept a man's action you can alter his results. Therefore do not judge either another man or yourself based on current failure and weakness. You can still change the process that propagated the outcome. A weakness is a result, but the action that produced the outcome of weakness can be altered to produce a different and desired outcome. One man's weakness today may be your strength tomorrow. This means a man can change his decision today to guarantee specific results that could benefit you tomorrow. If you require beauty as a result or an outcome become beautiful as an action. The main purpose of mistakes is to nurture absolution in the action. It is not the mistake that is important but the courage to act. Many people are just talkers. He who does one percent of what he said is far much better than he who talks a hundred percent and does nothing.

***

We are taught to live a life of limits by the so called realities that surround us every day. Though most people are not aware of this, we are limited in more ways than we would like to think and believe. Everyday hundreds if not billions of human beings are programmed mentally by television, radio and internet programs. We are programed just how far we can go, and where we are supposed to go. We are told how to get there and when, even being given the whys as well.

As you read this I believe you are reaching some level of awareness, which is a sign of truth. Truth must cause you to be more intentional and deliberate, assisting you not only in the discovery of your problems but also the dispensing of the solution. Problem discovered is problem potentially solved. Why tell me where to go and how far to go? Where is the adventure in that?

The Sky is the limit, that's' what we have all been taught but I refused from the moment I heard that to believe it. Something inside me naturally repelled that same statement. Fact becomes fact when you allow it to be so. You can always choose to have higher truth. I call it the principle of higher truth. It states that lesser truth can be replaced by higher truth always. Higher truth is superior to lesser truth. Past truth is important but not as important as current truth, for it is what you know now and act on that will elevate you. Past truth is history; current truth is the currency for the future.

CHAPTER TEN
FOCUS PAR EXCELLENCE

* * *

Brighton Ngarava

Focus a task at a time
***

Perfection should be everyman's pursuit, well at least everyone who seeks a different type of existence from the rest of the masses. Find something and commit to excel in that area no matter the cost. Pay the price for greatness; be willing to pay it without complaining. Great people are known for their willingness to go the full mile and get the job done. Everyone who is famous is famous for doing something so what will be your claim to fame and success. So many people want to succeed but not so many are willing to do what it takes to get there.

Many are strong starters but poor finishers. Remember the way you start is not as important as the way you finish. Most people start things and they don't finish what they start. Be committed to what you do, decide to be excellent at what you do, and then tirelessly work at it. I enjoy what I do; I can even forget to eat whilst doing it. Find that one thing and then perfect it. If excellence demands it then only concentrate on that one activity. This way all your energy will go into what you want to do and you will finish strong and have great results.

Do not waste all your energy on several things at the same time. Whether you are starting out or not simply stick to the regiment. If you take this route you will give an average input and get average outcomes because you will be divided between the activities you must do. You are not average, your pursuits deserve excellence and excellence is something we can all deliver otherwise it would not have been required of us.

Endeavour for Excellence
***

Excellence is the permanent mark of the great. The people you admire are those people who have a great level and sense of excellence. They are people who not only demand excellence from self but from those making their visions a reality.

When you are excellent in your thinking you demand and attract excellent things in your life. Excellent people attract excellent. Most things you encounter in your life you attract. It's just a matter of attraction in my own understanding of things. Whatever you decide to do make sure you do not try but rather do the best you can with everything you can master within yourself. Always make sure you accomplish what you set out to do in an excellent manner.

Whatever you put your hand to make sure you leave your mark there, make it a point to leave a mark of excellence, creativity and ingenuity. Be set apart, make your personal brand unique, leave 'your signature mark', or 'signature move', just make sure it is a positive mark. Be a trendsetter. Be the person that everyone else will want to emulate. Be the one everyone else wants to follow. Set out to be the Godfather of what you are known for.

Living in the level of excellence eliminates the competition that the rest of the crowd brings with them. When you decide to be excellent it means you have decided to live at a standard that only a few are privileged to experience.

There is another kind of a lifestyle that other people are living, a life where all things are excellence; a life where all things are expected to be excellent, a life where in its absence excellence is demanded. Come up and live that life, its better living from here than from down there.

Excellence is the lift that will get you to that level of life and it is the invitation that will gain you the pass to a new level in life. All I'm saying is that you have to make sure you get there; if you are already there make sure you stay there. These are things that only experience can best explain. Wealth, success and prosperity form part of those things. If you are to tell others of your success you must be able to point it out to them, for many people believe only in what they see. It is only what you see that you must believe.

***

The world of excellence
***

I called it a world above the world where everybody else lives. This world we live in is not for people who are trying their hand in life. This world is structured in a way that it inevitably makes a path for people who know what they want, and how they want it. Know what you want then never compromise your standards. Your work is your reputation. You are as good as your work in this world. People look at what you did and then they judge you. When you do something leave no room for your critics and haters. When you decide to put you hand at something never compromise. Be the kind to turn all your critics and haters into followers. Have standards that are true to you.

I have refused to work with certain sloppy individuals in the past because it presented a real threat to my image and reputation. Never be sloppy. Sloppy people lose out on the big things in life and will never get a gig with the major players in the industry field.

This will ensure that each single task you accomplish is excellent. If anything you set out to do is not designed to be excellent or you do not plan to perform that task in an excellent manner then it is not worth doing. When you apply this principle you will create the kind of opportunities that will result in your success in the future; because you cannot fail if you are truly committed to only attaining excellent outcomes.

One of the secrets to excellence is enjoyment. Focus all your energies on one task at a time; this way you begin to enjoy what you are doing. Make it a point to enjoy what you are doing. If you concentrate on the task but still do not enjoy it this might be a sign that the task or activity is a means to an end or what you are focusing on is simply not what you are to be doing. However you might require doing certain tasks you do not like in order to reach the destiny that you would like to attain.

***

Life is to be thoroughly enjoyed; all of us only get one. Make sure you focus on the process of whatever you are doing to find enjoyment and fulfillment. This will fuel the fire and desire to everything you want to accomplish quicker and better. A right mental state will mean the free flow of positive energy, which will result in tremendous positive outcomes.

CHAPTER ELEVEN
MIND CONTROL

* * *

Feed on challenges
***

The further you want to get in life the more you must challenge yourself. When challenges happen to come without an invitation destroy them completely. At an early age I realized that the greatness in me would be challenged by people and circumstances attempting to suppress me but I also realized with great challenges come great victories. I stopped feeling sorry for myself and depressed about why the world hated me and why people I had been faithful to betrayed me.

Now I wait for challenges, I feed on them, I become stronger by them. Nothing will ever develop you more and faster than challenges. Challenges force you develop your mind, to shift your thinking and come up with solutions. Challenges strengthen your resolve and bring out the best in you because the process of dealing with challenges requires you to think at a greater level than which the problem was created. So your experience with new situations and problems makes you grow. Without challenges life would be very boring, depressing and even purposeless. In some cases challenges help you discover the problems you were born to solve; therefore challenges are necessary for every man who seeks to lead a quality existence and build a legacy. Do you want to be rich? Solve a problem. Do you want to be famous for the right reasons? Solve a problem. Always tune your eye and mind to see the opportunities in all your problems.

Observe What You Think; Influence and Ultimately Control Them
***

He who cannot control his mind cannot take a firm hold on his future. Your future is a manifestation of a series of images your mind has been subjected to. Any man unable to tame his mind is a brute beast waiting to self-destruct. Almost everyone on earth is in self-destruct mode because they don't know how to control the only resource that can build their lives. Communities have been built by human minds, whilst countries have been utterly destroyed by other minds. The mind is both a dangerous and beautiful creature.

How do you observe your thoughts?
***

You are in control of your mind. Your mind should not be in control of you. So don't let your mind dictate what you should do or how you should feel. Be real with yourself. Are you generally a jovial happy jolly person or you are a joy killer, sour and bitter? Self-evaluation is the key to making real progress in life. You best know yourself. You can lie to others but not to self, you can pretend to be something else to others but not to self. Be real with yourself only then can you evaluate where you truly are and the steps you need to take to reach to where you want to get to. When you look at other people what do you think about them. What do you think about yourself? Is that the most accurate depiction or it is influenced by contaminated thoughts.

How to Influence Your Thoughts
***

A mind is like a human body. When a human being gets really hungry he can in the worst of cases just eat the very next thing they can get their hungry hands on. That is the same thing that happens with your mind. If you do not feed your mind with choice quality food your mind will feed itself with a kind and type of food that it can get its hands on. The food that the mind feeds is information which includes but not limited to words, images and thoughts. To influence and change your mind you must exchange mis-information for right-information. Feed yourself the right kind of information.

The things you read in magazines and papers or the programs you watch on TV or the content you watch on the internet shape your thinking. The information you share with people and the information that they share with you, what value are all these things adding to your mind or they are simply putting your mind in greater problems by helping it stray away from what actually matters as far as the bigger picture is concerned. guard your thoughts and your mind from contaminates.

You must get rid of anything communicating wrong information to you including the people around you. This is why you cannot be accessible to everyone and be available for every social outing just for the sake of keeping up appearances and trying to fit in. Guard your mind, guard your thoughts, guard your time, be careful who you associate with because a man can only be as good as his associates.

How do you control your thoughts?
(Disengaging negative thoughts and engaging positive ones).
***

To avoid chaos in your mind resulting in chaos in the outside world, you should try to observe your thoughts. Once you start doing that, you will notice how many negative thoughts you get daily. Imagine if all that negative energy were positive energy.

By observing negative thinking you will be able to emotionally disengage from it. As a result, negative thinking will affect you less and you will notice that your days will get more peaceful and positive even in the midst of a turbulent time. You will have the assurance within self that everything will be alright.

Enjoy life today and everyday
***

Don't be uptight. Try to be as spontaneous as you can be. You truly have one life to live and you don't want to have regrets of what you have always wanted to do or could have done but didn't do. Never be a serious person when it is not required of you, however be serious and committed to making yourself happy. Be approachable and be loveable. Be a master of balance. A life without balance is not balanced at all. There is no greater imbalance than imbalance.

The majority of people do not live in the present. They either camp in their past where they make frequent visits. People forget that the most important moment is now. Yesterday is history, today is opportunity and tomorrow is but a mystery out of our control. So the only moment more important is the present, the now. Absence in presence is either presence in past or future. Your presence in your past will only serve to pull you backward, but your presence in the future will pull you forward.

Many people spend their time in their past failure and disappointments. Never bring your past into your present; it might sneak unawares into your future and relive past events. Live in the present a little while and much in the future. The present is already passing; only the future is worth looking to for it is where you will live if you survive today. Why therefore meet the future when it comes; meet the future today so that when it comes you will know what it is for you have known today what it looks like.

You cannot afford not to live in the present. There is nothing more inspiring than living in the present. Be present in the present. Never be absent in the present. Absence in the present is absence in the future. Your current state of mind, exuberance and energy for life is important, be the life of the party or at least be present at the party if you can't be the life of it.

***

You have the power to determine just how great or horrible your day can be, you create the atmosphere for what you want and expect your day to be like. And your day becomes exactly that. You have been creating some of the things that happen to you, you have been a facilitator of some of the events that happen during your day without you even knowing it. The fact that you do not know you have been creating what happens around you and unconsciously shaping the process of your day and its outcome does not change the fact that you have been engaging in the creative process on a frequent and regular basis. Ignorance just isn't an excuse. Everything that happens to you is a sum total of your thoughts and what you subconsciously believe that you deserve. Now that you are conscious of the creative process of which you have long been a part of you can determine through certain variables just how your day will pan out. You should from now on wake up, tell yourself the kind of day you are going to experience, speak to yourself, 'I'm going to have a great day today', ;I'm going to enjoy my day today', 'Today is a great day', 'I'm enjoying this moment here and now', and you will begin to feel a difference within you. The change you want to see around you will start within you. You cannot change the world without changing yourself first.

Worrying
***

Do not focus on what you cannot change. Never ever focus your energies on what you cannot change. You can never change an outcome by focusing on it. Rather focus only on what you can change. What is it that you can change? You can change the processes that influence the outcomes. The reason why many people are in the situations they are or where they find themselves in and why they remain there is because of the fact that they worry about what they cannot change. Being where you are is an outcome, it is the result of processes that you messed up but from the ashes where you sit you can rise by making the right kind of choices that will create the right outcomes for you. For example you should never focus on the things you cannot change; those things that happen to you and people who backstab or betray you.. Those are outcomes of past experiences and processes which you may not have had an influence in altering or they were just wrong influences in your life. From now on focus on what you have in your hands for that is what carries the ability to change your current circumstance and create opportunities for your desired future. Something practical is daily relationship with say your spouse, partner, boss or colleague. If you do not like for example how your boss treats you or speaks to you it will most likely affect your morale thereby affecting your performance which will ultimately affect the quality of your results. The qualities of your results are therefore not caused by the way your boss treats you but rather by how you chose to react or respond to the way in which you are being treated. Do not react but rather respond. When you react you lose reason within your action. When you respond you assess the best possible action from that moment going forward that will optimize your results and give you maximum leverage out of your encounter. So though you were not able to determine what you encountered you determined how to respond and what the outcome would become. Your desired result should determine all current and necessary action. The great respond whilst weak react. Reactions are emotion filled actions with often disastrous endings; responses are thoughtful filled actions with desired endings. Wars have been started as a reaction and millions have died. Countries have been preserved as a response and millions of lives have been preserved. This is the story throughout history and this is the story of everyone's life. All current action determines future outcome. I think any man is as good as his reaction or response. From both these you can determine what manner of man you are dealing with; whether he is rational or irrational.

If you want to know who you truly consider yourself when confronted with frustrating situations, or encounters that are out of the grasp of your control; how you either react or respond to them is an indicator whether you are in shortfall or abundance. Actions, thoughts, behaviors, words when released create a sequence of events that will bring results which I call consequences. You can choose how you behave, speak or think but you cannot choose the consequences of those actions. You can choose your actions but never your consequences. Now if everything you do has an outcome you cannot change consequences. Why is it easy to believe that these principles and laws only apply as far as negative issues are concerned? I mean people are stern believers in suffering and punishment than they are of reward, blessing and prosperity. The same applies on both opposite ends of the spectrum of consequences and destiny. If you have a dream and goal you are at all costs willing to see through, you will focus on that end result and treat everything which is not in line with what you want to accomplish as an attempt at obstructing you from what matters the most. The people you come across, the complex situations you find yourself in are all out of your control, or at least the most of them but you have the power to shape those experiences into learning opportunities for your life. They make up the story of who you are. Success without a story is unsatisfying. Success without a story is meaningless, at least to me. By the time I reach my pinnacle in life and in my career I want to be able to tell someone else a story or write a book about it because I know someone else out there will be depending on my testimony to get the strength they need to persevere in their pursuits. You can be who you have always wanted to be. Go be exactly that and more.

ABOUT THE AUTHOR

Born in Harare, Zimbabwe. The author is a
personal development practitioner who advises and
coaches professionals and business people across different
industry sectors. His passion for empowerment is what drives
him to actively seek the growth and establishment of all he
comes across.

The Author has various other titles which include,
'Design Your Future',
'100% Happier You',
'The Practice of Success'.

Has this book impacted you in any way ?
Would you like to see the author speaking live about this book ?

Bookings – Conference/Keynote

Speaking/Engagements/Consultancy and Seminars - Contact

Email : brightonngarava@gmail.com
Call : +27733477550

Thank you for buying and/or reading this book.

www.ingramcontent.com/pod-product-compliance
Lightning Source LLC
Chambersburg PA
CBHW021407170526
45164CB00002B/544